E 70

SUCCESSFUL MARKETING TO U.S. HISPANICS AND ASIANS

Players, Agencies, and Media

AN AMERICAN MANAGEMENT ASSOCIATION RESEARCH REPORT ON

TARGET MARKETING

AMA Briefings & Surveys

Eric Rolfe Greenberg, Project Director
Yvette DeBow, Project Co-Director
Anne Skagen, Associate Editor
Diane Kraut, Staff Writer
Don L. Bohl, Managing Editor

Library of Congress Cataloging-in-Publication Data

Successful Marketing to U.S. Hispanics and Asians

   (AMACOM briefings & surveys)
    1. Hispanic Americans as consumers—United States.
2. Asian Americans as consumers—United States. 3. Market
surveys—United States. 4. Advertising campaigns.
I. American Management Association. II. Series.
HC110.C6S82 1987   658.8'348   87-27058
ISBN 0-8144-3514-9

This Research Report has been distributed to all members enrolled in
the Marketing Division of the American Management Association. Copies
may be purchased at the following single-copy rates: AMA members, $90.00.
Nonmembers, $100.00

© 1987 AMA Membership Publications Division,
American Management Association, New York, New York.
All rights reserved. Printed in the United States
of America.

Exhibits 6.3 through 6.17, © 1986, L3 Advertising, Inc.
All rights reserved. Used by permission.

This publication may not be reproduced, stored in a
retrieval system, or transmitted in whole or in part,
in any form or by any means, electronic, mechanical,
photocopying, recording, or otherwise, without the
prior written permission of AMA Membership
Publications Division, 135 West 50th Street,
New York, New York 10020.

First Printing

ISBN 0-8144-3514-9

Contents

		Highlights and Conclusions	5
The Hispanic Market	1	Understanding the Hispanic Market	9
	2	The Hispanic Agencies	14
	3	Players in the Hispanic Arena	22
	4	Hispanic Media	40
	5	Met Life: Across the Board	66
The Asian Market	6	Understanding the Asian Market	79
	7	Players in the Asian Market	97
	8	Asian-Language Media	104
	9	Focus on an Asian-Language Agency	116

HIGHLIGHTS AND CONCLUSIONS

AMERICA remains a nation of immigrants. The compass points, however, have shifted dramatically. Once, most immigrants came westward across the Atlantic. It was a journey of hope for most whites, of despair for most blacks—but the western horizon marked the way.

In the latter half of the 20th century, the direction has been northward across the Caribbean or over the Rio Grande, or eastward across the Pacific. The inevitable changes in American demography will be no less significant, in the long run, than those wrought by earlier waves of immigrants.

Projections are only that: educated guesses about growth patterns, fertility and mortality rates, geographic distributions and income patterns. But inexorably, Americans of Hispanic and Asian heritage will represent an ever-increasing percentage of the American body politic—and the American home market. And to the marketer, today offers opportunities to seed brand loyalties which will bear impressive fruit in the years to come.

The following research is based on approximately 100 interviews with persons associated with Asian and Hispanic target marketing: advertising directors, account managers, media spokespersons, and the like. Our objective was to search out elements of "success formulas"—tactics and commitments that seem to put a company in a winning position. For the Hispanic market, the principles proved easy to identify:

- *Homework.* Rather than complain about inaccurate media and U.S. Census figures, marketers have gone after numbers they needed. For most of the persons interviewed, information from

Strategy Research Corporation provided a point of departure for extensive proprietary research, especially focus groups and in-person interviews. One common finding: Large segments of the Hispanic community are best reached with Spanish language advertising.

- *Spanish literacy.* How the ad plays in Spanish is all important: "Walter Cronkite Spanish—not border Spanish." Inept copywriters have already run up an impressive list of bloopers, including unwanted sexual innuendoes in adds for chickens and sneakers. Virtually all successful campaigns have had key players of Hispanic origin as part of the team, either at the agency or in corporate. This ties closely with the next point.

- *Sensitivity to Hispanic culture, values, and lifestyles.* On the simplest level, this means identifying higher per-capita consumption in some product categories, such as soft drinks and fast foods. At times, the approach borders dangerously on stereotypes. "There's no secret about a Spaniard's love for a tall, cool drink," one product manager told our interviewer. On another level, this means getting in step with deeper values and important traditions. Consider, for example, J.C. Penney's *Quinceañera* gowns, or the personal letters from Delicioso's bear (Chapter 3).

- *Special services.* Spanish speaking persons on the 800 lines or at the service desk, Hispanic distributors and sales representatives, consumer education brochures, shopping guides, and credit card applications in Spanish, and the like.

- *Commitment—time and money.* It would seem logical for advertising directors to earmark about 9 percent of budget for this target segment, equating campaign budgets with general population statistics. A few of the larger, more recent initiatives are doing just that. The general rule, however, is to budget far less—especially if the company has been in the market for a while. "I won't tell you how little I'm spending," said one respondent. "You'd laugh at me if I did." (The product in question has been marketed to Hispanics for ten years, and commands the largest market share in its category.) Respondents agree, however, that it takes time—at least 18 months to two years—to gain any kind of critical mass.

- *Community presence.* The most successful campaigns are marked by a comprehensive or balanced approach, creating a product presence in the marketplace and a corporate presence in the community. This is one ingredient of McDonald's triumph over Burger King. See also the case study for Adolph Coors Company, Chapter 3.

The media landscape is changing. Turmoil in Hispanic television—takeovers and shifting alliances—can cause confusion for media buyers. Simultaneously, the print arena is moving toward unification, with a welcome network for national buys fresh on the scene. In any event, successful marketers will likely continue to put most of their budgets into local media, focusing on population concentrations, according to our respondents.

WILL THESE PRINCIPLES TRANSLATE INTO CHINESE?

Asian-Americans are now increasing at a rate faster than Hispanic Americans, with the Chinese being (at present) the largest national group. Successful campaigns to date suggest that the same approach may work. But this is largely an untapped market, and there is still much to be learned. Among our findings:

- For many product categories, Chinese Americans have yet to form brand awareness and brand loyalties, according to recent market research.

- Many marketers seem ill-informed about major product and service needs as well as cultural values and traditions. For example, the higher household headcounts and incomes would suggest an excellent market for large-ticket household goods. As of this writing, however, no U.S. corporation has entered this market. Many of the respondents interviewed were at a loss to tell us how marketers might play to festivals, celebrations, family traditions.
- Persons buying space and time in Asian media are getting one of the best possible bargains. The largest campaigns are working off of budgets in the $300,000 to $500,000 range.

Current campaigns in financial services and life insurance, telephone service, and packaged goods merit careful watching. Again, the most promising of these base promotion on sensitive and thorough research, put products into a cultural framework, work with community and civic groups, include Asian nationals as key team members, and the like. Again, it takes time. Results won't come in three months—as several of our respondents (mulling over less than successful campaigns) told us.

Further generalizations are difficult, and the reader is invited to look carefully at the case studies and other materials and form his or her conclusions.

Companies active in second-language marketing hold their cards close to the vest. Information on expenditures and buy patterns for space and time, and the conceptual framework surrounding their decisions, is not easily obtained. Many marketing managers spoke to AMA only on a not-for-attribution basis. The reason: those active in the arena feel that they hold an important competitive advantage, and are not eager to share their knowledge with the competition.

Publishers and station managers who sell space and time see a darker side to the secrecy. Already unhappy that their audience is undercounted by standard research methods, they fear that an unspoken agreement exists among advertisers to under-buy in second-language media and to keep rates artificially low. They wonder why major national accounts ignore the opportunities offered by Hispanic and Asian-language media. The frustration is high, and it tempers expectations for the future.

On the other hand, marketers have discovered that money put into alternative promotion (event marketing, support for dealers) pays a high return.

ORGANIZATION

Chapters 1 through 4 focus on the Hispanic market. First, general information about the size and dynamics of the market. Next, a look at major agencies and players in the market. Then, information on the media. Chapters 6 through 9 deal with the Asian market, using very much the same structure. Sandwiched between these two sections, by way of transition, is a case study of one company that has achieved success in both Hispanic and Asian-language markets.

Our deepest thanks and appreciation to those individuals who provided information to our researchers.

All products and services mentioned by name in this report are included to provide representative information. No endorsement is intended or implied.

1
Understanding the Hispanic Market

NO ONE questions the fact that a large and growing Hispanic market exists in the United States. The attraction: an identifiable subgroup of sufficient size to justify national campaigns, clustered into markets that are easy to target via local print and broadcast media.

The question: have they sufficient disposable income to make the effort worthwhile? *Aren't the Hispanics with significant amounts of disposable income reached with mainstream advertising?* Why spend money on pages in *El Diario* or time on Univision when you're already penetrating through *Cosmopolitan* and CBS?

One answer: pride. A sense of worth. A message that the ethnic culture is valued, that brand-name marketers and distributors consider the Hispanic cultural heritage a positive value.

Another answer: economy. There is more than self-interest at work when Hispanic broadcasters petition the Arbitron Corporation and organize an independent study of their audience. Like publishers of Spanish-language newspapers and magazines, they offer advertisers a bargain—commercial time and ad space at a cost-per-thousand far below not only English-language rates, but also Asian-language CPMs. The argument has to do with how great a bargain advertisers receive. Spanish-language ad rates offer significant cost savings even if Arbitron's figures are correct; if Arbitron undercounts the audience, as seems likely, the savings are all the higher.

THE COUNTING HOUSE

"How Many Hispanics?" asked the May 1987 issue of *American Demographics*, and proceeded to bundle the answers in a package of assumptions—not their own, but those of the U.S. Census Bureau. The assumptions had to do with growth rates: "The Bureau developed 30 projection scenarios based on different assumptions about Hispanic fertility, mortality, and immigration," the magazine reported. But assumptions about growth begin with the present population base, and therein lies a primary problem.

"Although the nation's 18 million Hispanics form the second-largest minority in the U.S., they are one of the least understood segments of the population for two reasons," *American Demographics* reported. "First, no one knows how many illegals cross the border. Second, no one knows how many Americans of Hispanic descent do not identify themselves as 'Hispanic' on census forms."

Immediately, then, the base number of 18 million becomes questionable. In the same issue of *American Demographics*, a separate story on Hispanic brand loyalty leads with the statement, "The 19 million Hispanics in the U.S. are a brand-conscious, brand-loyal market...." In 20 pages the current Hispanic population has grown by one million.

About one thing there is no argument: the domestic Hispanic population is growing at a rate far greater than the national norm. Of the various scenarios prepared by the U.S. Census Bureau, the *lowest* projected growth rate for Hispanics over the next quarter-century is 57 percent (the highest is 133 percent). Compare this with the projected growth of the total U.S. population: 18 percent over the same quarter-century. Juggle the figures as you will; any way you read them, the Hispanic population represents an ever increasing percentage of the home market.

Changes *within* the Hispanic population present another volatile factor. High fertility rates drive down the median age, while at the other end of the scale a longer life expectancy brings it back up again. The Census Bureau's *Projections of the Hispanic Population: 1983 to 2080* foresees greater increases in middle-aged and older Hispanics than in children and young adults: the report lists the 1985 median age at 24.7 years, increasing to 25.6 by 1990, 27.0 by 2000, and 28.2 by 2010. The rise portends a greater segment of wage-earners within the group, with obvious implications for average disposable income—even if such factors as mainstream assimiliation and increasing levels of education are not considered.

"Hispanics made $84.8 billion in aggregate after-tax money income during 1984," said *Hispanic Business* in its review of Census Bureau statistics, noting an annual increase of 12.5 percent from 1980 figures. "Hispanic purchasing power is expected to reach $172 billion by 1990, if the 1980-1984 trend is any indication." And is it any indication? The Census Bureau's 1985 report boosted the aggregate to $93.4 billion, an increase of 10 percent—a lesser rate of increase than the previous five-year average. More seriously, the later report showed an actual *decrease* of 0.4 percent in the mean after-tax income of Hispanic households, which declined to $17,920 in 1985 from $17,978 in 1984.

How can the aggregate income increase while mean household incomes decrease? By a simultaneous increase in the number of households. Hispanics are spending more dollars—but there are more Hispanics spending them. The 1985 figures reveal that Hispanics represent an ever larger slice of the American pie, while more households are demanding a bite out of that slice.

"More" is the operative word. *Hispanic Business* chose a middle-series set of assumptions from the Census Bureau's 30 scenarios, matched it against projections for the black population, and constructed a "best guess" which shows that Hispanics will overtake blacks as the nation's largest minority group in the year 2015. In 1985, Hispanics represented seven percent of the U.S. population; by 2010, that percentage will nearly double. "Looking further into the future with these assumptions," the magazine predicted, "the Hispanic population would number 99 million in 2080—28 percent of a total U.S. population of 355 million. Hispanics in this scenario would outnumber all other minorities combined (61 million blacks and 37 million 'others'), and they would be gaining rapidly on the 163 million white non-Hispanics."

PRESENT TENSE

But while they gain in numbers, what will they lose in ethnic identification? In 1880, the largest ethnic stock in the American population, after the English, were the Germans; that remains true today, a century later, but they speak no German, read no German newspapers, tune in to no German broadcasts. Marketers, who in any case must sell goods and services today and tomorrow, not a hundred years hence, must exercise a fine judgment. What considerations, beyond sheer numbers of the present and future, justify Spanish-language marketing activity today?

The *1987 U.S. Hispanic Market Study,* published by the Miami-based Strategy Research Corporation (SRC), is packed with helpful insight. More than 2,000 interviews in 21 markets yielded data to show that assimilation is a slow process, and far from a reality for a significant segment of the Hispanic community. Relevant data from SRC study:

Language. Seven out of ten SRC respondents reported speaking only Spanish at home; another 18 percent speak both Spanish and English. A majority speak Spanish "on social occasions"; one-third speak Spanish at work.

Less than half of SRC's interview subjects thought highly of their ability to read English: 42.1 percent said they read English "very well" or "well," and 21.9 percent said they did not read English at all. Conversely, 80 percent said they read Spanish "well" or "very well."

"Virtually nine out of every ten U.S. Hispanics first learned to speak Spanish," the SRC report reads. "Overall, English was the first language spoken by only 6.4 percent of all respondents interviewed."

There were regional variations in the statistics. For example, 35.5 percent of Hispanics in the Southeast said they couldn't speak English, compared to 16.8 percent of the national sample and 12 percent of those in the Northeast. Country of origin also made a difference: 30.3 percent of the Cubans polled said they couldn't read English, against just 10.6 percent of the Puerto Ricans. And there were differences by age group as well, with the 18-34 segment more fluent and better able to read in English than their elders. But still, only 47.9 percent of the 18-34 group said they read English "very well" or "well," and 19.8 percent of that younger group said they couldn't read English at all.

Ongoing fluency in Spanish is encouraged: 85.8 percent of SRC's respondents said they considered it "very important" that the community's children have the ability to read and write Spanish. Figures remained remarkably constant across market segments and places of origin. The clear and consistent finding: Hispanics are, and will remain, attached to their language and to the cultural heritage it carries.

Identification. "Although they may have been living in the United States for many years and indeed are American citizens," the SRC study reports, "many U.S. Hispanics still adhere to the Spanish language, culture and traditions of their country of origin." To quantify the number of Hispanics who presently live in the U.S. as to their self identification, survey participants were asked, "How would you describe yourself?" The options were:

- Hispanic First/American Second
- Equally Hispanic and American
- American First/Hispanic Second

"Almost three-fourths of Hispanic-Americans think of themselves as 'Hispanic First/American Second,'" SRC found.

This time, there occured no major differentiation by country of origin: in fact, despite Puerto Rico's U.S. Commonwealth status, a higher percentage of Puerto Ricans (75 percent) described themselves as "Hispanic First/American Second" than Cubans (74.2 percent) or Mexicans (70.4 percent). There were, however, important regional variations, with Hispanics in the Southwest reporting a greater level of identification as "Americans" than elsewhere. "Hispanics in the Central region feel the strongest about their Hispanic background: 88.7 percent responded that they were 'Hispanic First/American Second,'" reported SRC. "This response is cited least frequently by Hispanic-Americans living in the Southwest region (63.8 percent)."

Social Attitudes. A whole series of statements designed to quantify social attitudes demonstrated over and over again a strong sense of ethnic solidarity. More than 90 percent of SRC's respondents agreed that they are "proud to be Hispanic" and think that their "culture, language and traditions should be preserved." Many more—83.9 percent—preferred listening to Latin music than to American music. In these matters of social attitude, SRC found that "age is not a factor in terms of how Hispanics feel about their heritage, culture and language and the preservation of these."

SRC did find that slight variances exist when comparing Hispanics under 55 years of age to those 55 years of age and older. Specifically, Hispanics 55 and older display a lower level of agreement with such attitudinal statements as "Socializing With American Friends," "Listening to American Music," and "Dancing to American Rhythm."

"Language fluency may be a factor contributing to this lower incidence of agreement among elderly Hispanics," the SRC report summarized.

Consumer Attitudes. SRC interviewers brought the question around to marketing concerns by presenting a series of statements and scoring the responses on a 1-to-5 scale, a one representing "total disagreement" with the statement, a five "complete agreement." These responses were measured against weighted average scores by a non-Hispanic sample. The results merit study by marketers. They show that nationally advertised brands have a special hold upon the Hispanic consumer, but that the hold is not unbreakable—Spanish shoppers are not convinced that they will continue to buy tomorrow the brands they use today. And, too, they respond wholeheartedly to the special consideration that Spanish-language marketing displays.

In degrees remarkably similar to non-Hispanics, Hispanic consumers agree with these statements posed by SRC interviewers:

- "Nationally advertised and popular name brands are superior in quality to store brands." On the 1-to-5 scale provided, Hispanic respondents averaged a 3.58 grade of agreement, compared to a 3.42 average among non-Hispanics.
- "Nationally advertised and popular name brands are the best products for my family." Hispanics scored a 3.58 average, non-Hispanics 3.46.

Newly-arrived immigrant groups, deprived of familiar homeland products, naturally gravitate toward brands they see blazoned upon billboards, hyped in the media, piped in their newspapers. Their choices are made easier by the international scope of American product marketing: American brands are a familiar presence in Latin American stores. Many Hispanics are presold on American goods and arrive with brand loyalty already at work.

But that loyalty is not unshakable. Consider SRC's responses to this statement:

- "The popular name brands I use most often today are going to be the same brands I will be using next year." While non-Hispanics agreed by a 3.84 average, Hispanics averaged just 3.28.

This half-point spread is unusual among SRC tabulations. The obvious implication: while nationally recognized brands are attractive to Hispanic consumers, their loyalties are not fixed with the same determination that non-Hispanics reveal. Marketers of consumer goods may claim that loyalty with targeted marketing campaigns. That statement is supported by SRC's further finding:

- "When shopping, I consider brands/companies which have shown interest and really appreciate the Hispanic community." Among Hispanics, the average level of agreement here was 3.70—higher than the average for any other statement regarding brand loyalty.

The obvious conclusion: opportunity is knocking—and the knock has a Latin rhythm. Products and services which seek out Hispanic consumers and speak to them in their own language can mark up significant gains in market share in an ever growing segment of the home market. That is the theory, supported by SRC's data. But as we will see, practice teaches the same lesson.

A GRANDSTAND VIEW

Thus the Hispanic-American community, its numbers, its attractions, its attitudes, according to recent research. But it is necessary to know more—knowledge that only practical experience can yield. In the sections that follow, we take a close-up look at actual practice, and the lessons and opinions that come from hands-on work. We watch the players in action on the field, listen to the agencies who coach those players, and hear from the broadcasters and publishers who provide the field of play. We invite the reader to keep score.

2

The Hispanic Agencies

THE DEMOGRAPHICS tell only part of the story. More important is real insight into Hispanic consumers—who they are and why they purchase specific products. To find out, AMA researchers went to the advertising agencies and asked what Hispanic consumers want and how marketers are going about delivering it to them. The biggest question: Is it really important to advertise to Hispanics in their native language?

WHO IS THE AVERAGE HISPANIC CONSUMER?

According to Mavis Cordero, a partner in the agency Muse Cordero Chen & Baca (a division of Mingo-Jones), the average Hispanic-American consumer is:

Female
From the southwest
Mexican
Twenty-two years old
From a family of approximately four persons
Living in a male-dominated society
From a strict home environment
Politically passive
Very proud of Hispanic heritage
Roman Catholic
Fluent in both Spanish and English, but preferring Spanish

Spending more on cosmetics and health aids than the average American

Influenced in brand preference by whether the advertisers address her as an Hispanic

Brand loyal

The last two points are echoed time and time again by those involved in the market. The consensus is that generic products don't work well. The Hispanic consumer is skeptical and believes that name-brand products are superior in quality. When a national advertiser moves into the market, Hispanic consumers take notice and try the product *if* they are unsatisfied with their current choice or have not developed a strong sense of loyalty to it.

But once Hispanics are satisfied with a product and believe that the company is interested in having their business, it is very difficult for another product to break through. This factor underscores the importance of entering the market quickly and beating out the competition.

Sy Davis, president of Adelante Advertising (clients: Alpo Pet Foods, Inc., American Cyanamid Co., Cafe Caribe, E & J. Gallo winery, Heinz Ketchup and Babyfood, New World Enterprises, Prudential Insurance, Remy Martin, Sunshine Biscuits; billings for 1986: $6.5 million), puts it this way: "The Hispanic market is changing. The transient character of the group no longer exists, as more immigrants are coming to the United States for political rather than economic reasons. The smart advertiser will see the potential in this market and, with the proper direction, will win over the Hispanic consumer for years to come."

Davis adds, "They are not fickle consumers, and it is very difficult to change them once they feel a brand is quality. If a company wants to gain a foothold in the market, to be one step ahead of the competition it must enter the market seriously and be ready to commit strong budgets to its success. Really, it's just good business sense."

MADE IN AMERICA

To Hispanics this label means quality. Whereas most Americans believe that better products are produced abroad, Hispanics prefer products that are American made. An Adelante pilot test for Combat, an insecticide manufactured by American Cyanamid, underscores this point. After screening t.v. spots, many of the viewers commented on the presence of the company name and copymark sign in the lower corner of the screen during the broadcast. The fact that the name of the parent company included the word "American" strengthened the perception of the product as superior.

Cordero concurred, pointing out that in South America, for instance, "Levi's are the hottest thing going. There is something about American products that they [Hispanics] go wild about."

DIFFERENT BACKGROUNDS, DIFFERENT METHODS?

As the demographics show, Hispanics of different origins live in different areas of the country. An elementary breakdown: Mexicans in the western, southwestern, and central states, Puerto Ricans in the central and northeastern states, and Cubans in the southeastern states. Central and South Americans are scattered among these regions, with most migrating toward the eastern part of the country. Most advertisers agree that by segmenting Hispanics into regions, subtleties can be added to campaigns to give the flavor of the region without much difficulty. According to Davis, these adaptations can be as simple as changing the background music.

For Cordero, differentiation among the groups is especially important when promoting a personal product. Personal hygiene products, for example, should be tailored to regions—say, a Puerto Rican woman in the Northeast—but products like soft drinks are more easily marketed by a generic type of advertising, as long as it's in Spanish.

Guy Antonioli, vice president/senior account supervisor for Campbell-Ewald Latina, Miami (clients: Eastern and Chevrolet; billings for 1986: $12.5 million), comments: "In the United States, most Hispanics are exposed to both Spanish and English media—their response depends on the level of assimilation. Take, for example, the Hispanic housewife. She spends most of her time at home, in an Hispanic community. In this environment she listens, watches, and reads Hispanic media—advertising to her should be in Spanish.

"On the other hand, the Hispanic businessman or woman spends a large percentage of his or her time in a non-Hispanic environment. When marketing to them, especially with high-ticket products such as cars or other luxury items, English-language media, using creative executions with an Hispanic flavor, can be as important as Spanish-language communications."

PROMOTION ADVERTISING

Although television, radio, and print are the big three advertising vehicles in terms of percentage of advertising budget allocations, advertisers also feel that the development of promotional programs is a significant tool in attracting the Hispanic consumer.

According to Sonya Suarez, director of Hispanic marketing for Fraser-Smith, Inc., in New York (clients: Miller Brewing Company and McDonald's), "Promotion is an important marketing vehicle used to reach and impact the Hispanic consumer market. Specifically, event marketing allows you to touch base with the Hispanic community on a grassroots level, impacting those segments of the Hispanic consumer market that can be missed when using only Spanish-language media.

"Successful event marketing in the Hispanic consumer market oftentimes uses sports and/or music-oriented promotional centerpieces which provide a broad-based appeal to all the Hispanic subgroups."

An example of a promotional campaign that is enjoying success in the New York metropolitan area is "Festival Latino," organized by Great Events Promotion of Great Neck, New York. The concept: combining coupon savings with a sweepstakes package. When customers use the coupons they will automatically be registered in the sweepstakes, where they can win valuable prizes: cars, trips, and televisions.

Coupons are generally unfamiliar to Hispanic communities. On the other hand, sweepstakes events are

The Hispanic Agencies

very popular in Hispanic homelands such as Puerto Rico. By combining the two, advertisers can change and create perceptions about the couponing process. Many Hispanics perceive coupons in the same light as food stamps and are embarrassed to use them in their local grocery stores. This concept helps to teach them that coupons can reduce the prices of their favorite brand-name products.

For advertisers, Festival Latino is an ideal vehicle to bring products into the Hispanic community. Circulation for the latest event (July 1987) was at 1.5 million households within the tri-state area of New York, New Jersey, and Connecticut. Besides offering the manufacturer's product exclusivity, the event also provides radio, magazine, and transit promotional advertising.

Another company that distributes coupons among the Hispanic community is Carol Wright. Davis believes that this form of advertising has a positive impact on the market. The products he represents receive a 5 percent return on the coupons. And this 5 percent is very respectable—especially since the concept is relatively unknown. According to Tony Mercado, who handles the Carol Wright Hispanic advertising for Donnelley Marketing, for Anglos the redemption rate on Carol Wright products is 10.5 percent, whereas on all coupons in general it is 9 percent.

The Carol Wright Hispanic program reaches approximately 2.8 million households. It began in 1980 as a result of client pressure and currently goes into 70 Hispanic markets. Initially 8 brands participated in the program and, within six years, representation has increased to 92. These are primarily national-brand advertisers, and Donnelly's benchmark is a 67 percent repeat business rate on clients. According to Davis, "If the message is clear, and the incentive is correctly directed toward the Hispanic consumer, he or she will respond."

OUTDOOR ADVERTISING

Billboard, eight-sheet, and mass-transit poster advertising are additional ways for consumer-goods manufacturers to attract the Hispanic consumer. According to Antonioli, "Billboard and eight-sheet advertising can be most cost effective in high-density Hispanic communities."

The size and scope of a billboard is enough to influence the Hispanic consumer, or any consumer for that matter, but the eight-sheet boards, as Davis sees it, add to retailers' point-of-purchase displays. "The eight-sheet outdoor posters, which are approximately one-third the size of the standard billboard display, are viewed by the pedestrian, usually near the retailer. We find this to be the most useful. Because of this proximity, we actually consider it to be one part of a two-part point-of-purchase sales effort."

In addition, Davis has also worked in the area of mass-transit advertising, using smaller size posters with "take-one" cards for clients that include New World Enterprises, Cafe Caribe, and Sunshine Biscuits.

MARKETING STRATEGY

When developing a marketing strategy, all the respondents agree that there is really no difference between marketing to Anglos and to Hispanics. The agency uses the same tools and approaches that constitute creative and effective advertising for both. The idea is that good "creative" transcends all language barriers.

According to Antonioli, "Marketing expertise should, and here does, transcend language groups. When preparing advertisements for our clients, we outline our advertising strategy and develop materials (composed of factual information) to respond to our clients' consumers. All of the traditional tools are used."

Antonioli's formula is based on information developed around four existing variables:

- Budget
- Target audience
- Product
- Market

"Wanted" Posters?

The pitfalls of cross-cultural translation nearly tripped up National Car Rental's Spanish-language campaign in Miami and New York, recalls Lewis Carbone, then with National's agency and now their vice president for marketing communications.

Although the word "American" has strong positive connotations for Hispanic consumers, the word "national" often gives off extremely negative vibrations—especially to Latins whose homelands have known dictatorial rule. In English the word is politically neutral, with a meaning of "nationwide." In Spanish, however, *nacional* means "the state"—specifically, the national government and, often, the national police.

The car rental agency's slogan of "You Deserve National Attention" is a natural in English, with its dual implications of customer service and nationwide celebrity. But direct translation into Spanish brings with it an unsavory political undertone. In some Latin countries "national attention" is the last thing a citizen desires.

According to Carbone, the answer was to back the slogan with immediate reassurance—examples, visual and verbal, of kindly treatment by National operatives at airport rental booths and in telephone reservations. Thus the campaign leapt the cultural wall, selling the company's service while at the same time educating Hispanic immigrants in the new realities of the American political scene.

The rental service used the same space ads in Latin American countries, spotting them in vehicles appropiate for tourist advertising. Carbone cites the campaign as an important element in transforming National Car Rental from an operations-oriented culture to a market-driven one.

And no one was arrested.

"Spanish-language ads should complement their English-language counterparts. The execution can be different, but they should communicate the same ideas and benefits," insists Antonioli.

When developing these ads, the emphasis is as much on information as it is on entertainment. According to Davis, "The Hispanic consumer is not as cynical as the Anglo. The media use less entertainment in advertising to the Hispanic market, per se, than in the general market. The emphasis is more on informing consumers—teaching them about the products, their uses and benefits."

Translation is another area where marketing strategy comes into play. Too many times companies make the mistake of translating the Anglo campaign directly into Spanish—and often with embarrassing outcomes. For example, a leading marketer of poultry placed an ad that, in Spanish, read: "It takes a viral/sexy man to make a chicken affectionate." Not exactly what it was intended to say.

All those concerned stress that proper translation is essential in producing effective creative for the Hispanic media. What is needed is not direct translation, but an Hispanic way of saying what you mean.

TYPES OF PRODUCTS

The crucial point to remember is that in the Hispanic perception of things brand-name equals quality. And quality is equated with assimilation.

According to Davis, "Proportionally, dollars spent in the supermarket are much greater with the Hispanic consumer than the general market. The Hispanic values quality food, personal-care products, and the like. Their disposable income does not go to as great a variety of products and categories as that of the general market."

According to Cordero, products such as baby items, food, beer, soft drinks, and personal-care items are areas where marketers can benefit from the Hispanic consumer. But it is with the high-ticket items and brand-name products that the greatest advertising value comes in. "They want the best. For the most part, high-ticket items such as VCRs, televisions, and cars can be purchased more cheaply here than in their native countries, in addition to being of higher quality. With traditional consumer products, generics are perceived as being of inferior quality than their brand-name counterparts. By purchasing brand-name products, Hispanics get a feeling of assimilation—identification with the mainstream."

Davis concurs on this point. "They don't trust generics. This goes back to their heritage in Latin America. For the most part, Latin American countries were used as a dumping ground for seconds and poorly made products."

THE MEDIA: TELEVISION, RADIO, AND PRINT

In general, the broadcast media (television and radio) are the primary outlets for advertisers to the Hispanic market (See Chapter 4). The advantages of advertising via these media are clear in terms of penetration of the market and the number of viewers and listeners being reached, say agency spokespersons. But the print media is somewhat ignored. Why is this so, and is this trend changing?

Print, for the most part, takes a back seat to the broadcast media, basically because of an unfair stereotype that Hispanics don't read. Cordero sees it in a different light. "In general reading is a single function," she says, "it is something that you do on your own. Hispanics tend to spend their free time in group activities. Watching television or listening to the radio are more group events than reading."

But there is a definite change within the print media—which can be exemplified by the move of the *Miami Herald,* which is now researching ways to gain readership among the Hispanic residents in the Miami area.

THE FUTURE OF THE MARKET

According to Suarez, the differentiation in the Hispanic market (depending on the subgroup) should be more along the lines of generation, with assimilation occurring more among the children of the original immigrants. "Among the younger generation there is certainly a trend toward 'Americanization,' but as they get older, there's a certain turning back to the ethnic traditions. The older generation speaks little English. They're in neighborhoods where it simply isn't necessary to learn English. Most can get by if they have to, but most don't need English in their everyday lives. They may have the intention of moving back to the 'old country,' but after they've been here 35 to 40 years, and their children and grandchildren are here, the chances are they are not moving back."

On a different note Davis points to the newer immigrants, who have a greater desire to assimilate—more like earlier generations of immigrants from Europe. Then, most people came here to stay, unlike many of the Mexican immigrants, whose first impulse was to come here to make money in order to have a better life in Mexico when they returned.

"Because of the political problems in Central and South America we will begin seeing people coming here for political rather than economic reasons," according to Davis. "These are people who will be setting down roots, not looking to come here to make money and then go back to establish themselves. These are the consumers who the major consumer-goods manufacturers will have to address, simply because of their number and its effect on the consumption percentage. The company that comes in, promotes in the right way, and addresses the Hispanic market properly will be the company to reap the benefits."

ADVICE

What are a company's major considerations before getting involved in the market? We posed this question to our advertising experts, and the responses varied. According to Antonioli, it's not numbers running that is needed but an Hispanic way of thinking. "There is big potential in the market, but you must remember one important thing—to reap the potential you not only have to analyze the numbers, but you also need someone on staff who understands the Hispanic consumer—or a consultant or agency that can provide you with the expertise. Anyone can run the numbers, but not everyone can understand the market."

According to Suarez, three points need to be addressed in marketing to the Hispanic consumer. All three must also allow for the changing nature of the immigrant groups and the tools available to reach them.

"First, generic marketing alone does not work. There are prospective clients who talk as if it were 20 years ago. They feel that their mainstream advertising hits the entire market, that there is no need for special segments. Of course, Hispanics see mainstream advertising, but viewing a spot does not mean impacting. Special-segment efforts have a far greater impact.

"Second, translations or adaptations of mainstream campaigns rarely work, and, of course, they can get you into trouble. A direct translation of a recent Braniff campaign urged Hispanics to 'Fly with me and sit naked.'

"Third, understand the market. Hispanic consumers have a large degree of consumer loyalty and are both brand conscious and quality conscious. In effect, as a consumer group Hispanics are in the mainstream but they aren't best reached through mainstream messages."

Davis underscores the translation problem—which almost all the professionals involved in the market see as the area where the biggest mistakes are made, yet the easiest to solve. "The Hispanic community is usually offended by mistakes made due to poor translations; it shows neglect on the part of the advertiser. Thus it is important when one goes into Hispanic advertising to do it properly or not at all.

"You should do it not by translating the words specifically, but by converting the idea to appeal to the Hispanic way of thinking and to differentiate, when necessary, among the subsets within the group.

"Find an agency that can help you with your translations. It's not difficult to do, and it can produce a significant, positive effect on your Hispanic marketing effort."

3

Players in the Hispanic Arena

THIS CHAPTER presents detailed information on how a number of major corporations are making Hispanic marketing work. The case studies were selected to represent a variety of products and services, and to highlight approaches that seemed especially worthwhile. A closing section provides generalized insights from respondents who asked that their company names not be disclosed.

COORS: LOYALTY IS A TWO-WAY STREET

Adolph Coors Company has made an unprecedented commitment to the U.S. Hispanic community. Its efforts in Hispanic advertising, promotion, and community relations are far-reaching, to the tune of $60 million in 1986 alone. Its aim: to create not just a market but a corporate presence in the Hispanic marketplace. Its vehicle: the Hispanic Agreement, providing for some one hundred programs ranging from special events throughout the country to scholarship awards, contributions, distributorships.

How can this be good business when for many companies the bottom line is staying alive in a troubled economy? Coors finds not only that the Hispanic market is a lucrative one but also that Hispanics have a contribution to make to the company.

A Partnership Approach

"It's not a charity package," declares Frank Solis, national program manager of Coors' community relations department. "We feel that it's good business. We're taking money out of the community, and we feel we have a corporate responsibility to put money back into that community. To us, the community is our partner.

"If we're going to go out and buy tires or widgets, why not buy them from an Hispanic supplier of tires or widgets? They're out there, too. I think all too often in corporate America that's overlooked."

The Hispanic Agreement, signed in 1984 with a coalition of Hispanic organizations, represented the largest single corporate commitment ever made by a U.S. company to the Hispanic community. The five-year package has a value of $350 million.

The agreement states: "Adolph Coors Company attempts to represent the best of what our country stands for—opportunity, diversity, and freedom. Our company has a history of commitment dedicated to opportunity for all people, and that includes the hiring and promotion of Hispanic employees, business associations with Hispanic suppliers and financial institutions, as well as contributions to Hispanic support groups."

In response to this agreement, Coors has set up a significant number of Hispanic-owned distributorships. In fact, half of all American Hispanic-owned distributorships fly Coors' banner. For contributions, Coors has set aside a half-million dollars a year for this benefit alone, as well as 9 percent of its procurement dollars for Hispanic vendors in 1987. Two years ago the total expenditure to Hispanic suppliers was $600,000. Last year it reached $60 million. With such programs, and others such as cash deposits to Hispanic-owned banks, Coors is putting its best foot forward.

The Target

Coors has targeted legal-drinking-age (LDA) Hispanics up to age 34 as its primary Hispanic market, with Hispanics age 35 to 49 as its secondary market. This contrasts with the general market target audience. For the general market, Coors' advertising targets only extend up to age 34. Research in the Hispanic market has indicated that there is a significant beer-consumption trend among older Hispanics that is not seen in the general market.

Is targeting the Hispanic market a smart move on the part of Coors? The answer is unquestionably yes. Coors' own research shows that the Hispanic per-capita consumption index is higher than that of the general market. The latter is 100; the Hispanic consumption averages about 140. For further comparison, the black consumption index is about 89. By targeting Hispanics in their ADIs, Coors reaches more beer consumers than it does in its other segments. Thus, for Coors, the Hispanic market is indeed a lucrative one.

Coors subsegments the market in two ways. Nationality groups constitute a subsegment, with differentiation among Mexicans, Cubans, Puerto Ricans, and the like. These groups have very subtle differences, be it linguistics, lifestyle, or geographical area. The other type of subsegmentation takes assimilation patterns among Hispanics into account (a distinction many companies fail to make).

Many Hispanic consumers watch mainstream television, but do not relate to its commercial messages the way that non-Hispanics do. Ads with blond-haired, blue-eyed actors do not always create a sense of product preference among Hispanics. And in states such as Texas, New Mexico, Colorado and

California, which were originally part of Mexico, Hispanic residents are primarily American-born people who still identify heavily with the Hispanic tradition. In response to this, Coors has created a series of commercials to be aired on mainstream television, in English, featuring Hispanic actors.

According to Solis, "We feel that the consumer has to be able to identify with both the product and the company." This two-pronged strategy has led to Coors' comprehensive approach, geared toward product-oriented activities on the one hand, and corporate-oriented activities on the other. A proper balance between the two characterizes Coors' presence in the Hispanic marketplace and accounts for its success over the last decade.

Product Orientation

Coors sponsors a multitude of special events that offer consumers a unique opportunity to sample its product. One such event takes place in Miami each October, and targets the gamut of Hispanic nationalities that have made that city an Hispanic center.

The 1986 Miami event, called "Discovery of America Day," was coordinated by the Hispanic Heritage Festival Committee, and drew a crowd of more than 20,000 people. The event re-enacted the disembarking of Christopher Columbus with his crew of Conquistadores, accompanied by Fernando and Isabella, all dressed in period costumes.

Entertainment by Argentinian, Puerto Rican, Cuban, and other Latin groups included music and dance, and was continued throughout the day. Traditional Hispanic foods, as well as Coors beer, enhanced the festivities. Says Solis, "There are a lot of people out there who, prior to these special events, have never sampled our product.

"We feel that by providing events in an environment where people can attend free or for a reasonable price (for the benefit of the community) everybody wins."

Special events sponsored by Coors cover the entire spectrum, from boxing to softball to dances to concerts.

Measuring Success

According to Solis, "The only true way you can measure success in that market is by taking a look at what percent of your business is done there. It's very hard to arrive at any share of market vis-a-vis competitors. With distributorships, there are so many territorial overlaps and so many multibrand companies that you're never going to really get a precise figure on what your share of market is in a particular state."

Coors conducts an array of market research. In fact, Solis declares that they have become almost fanatical about it over the last few years. "From independent research companies to in-house research, we try to cover everything. Focus groups, door-to-door polls, molinar sets, television surveys. If it measures the market, we've used it." The questions Coors puts to consumers are categorized as advertising recall, unaided brand recall, brand preference (first and second choices), and brand avoidance.

Corporate Advertising

Corporate advertising provides Coors with a vehicle for leveraging its participation in a variety of Hispanic community events. It presents the activities and programs in which Coors is involved across the country.

Last year Coors spent roughly $15 million in advertising to the Hispanic consumer. This included everything from special events to t.v., radio, and print, including a mainstream television campaign featuring Hispanics in positive roles. Considered alone, Spanish-language advertising amounts to 8 or 9 percent of the total media budget.

Insights

Solis sums it up: a company has to make a firm decision and stick with it. "The first couple of years have to be viewed as investment spending. I've seen instances where companies have gone into the marketplace with a splash, only to pull out 180 days later. In each target market that a company selects, I think it has to formulate a corporate strategy that emphasizes maintaining a constant presence in the marketplace, to a point where new ads are breaking on the average of every six to eight weeks. Be it on a large scale or small scale, someone will be talking positively about the company and the products in the marketplace." The time frame: "We're talking about one and a half to two years, just to set a benchmark."

DELICIOSO

This is the case of the product that did so well, it knocked itself right out of the market.

The product in question is Delicioso, a powdered soft-drink created by Amstar Corporation (the makers of Domino products). Adelante's strategy was so successful that the product began to steal market share from another soft drink marketed by the parent company.

When Amstar first came up with the idea of marketing a fruit-flavored powdered drink mix to the Hispanic market, it approached the Adelante agency in New York City. A company with long experience in the Hispanic market arena (see the chapter on Hispanic agencies), Adelante took up the challenge. The marketers settled down to do their homework on the soft-drink market, which included investigating potential Hispanic interest in such a product.

The pressing question: How will the Hispanic consumer respond to a powdered soft-drink mix made especially for them? The answer: very well.

The Homework

According to Sy Davis, president of Adelante, there were two audiences that needed to be targeted for this particular product. The first was the adult—more specifically Mom, who would be the purchaser of the product. The second was the child, who would be the consumer—particularly children between the ages of 6 and 11. Market research had shown that after age 11, children are more interested in those products which are packaged in bottles or cans than those in powdered form.

What's in a Name? Identification

Their first strategy, after identifying the market, was to develop a name and identity for the product. Adelante's team came up with *Delicioso,* meaning "delicious" in English. This name also created an identifiable personality for the product, because *oso* means "bear" in Spanish. At that point they had a product with a name (Delicioso), an identifiable personality (a bear), a package (cannisters and packets), and a range of fruit flavors from tropical and cherry to orange and grape.

The Research

To gain the information on packaging and consumer identity, as well as to develop a character for the bear, Adelante conducted focus groups in five Hispanic areas: Los Angeles, New York, Miami, San Antonio, and Chicago. The groups were broken into two segments, one consisting of adults, the other of children. Adelante was looking for information on appeal and packaging, and a clue as to how products sell to Hispanic consumers in different parts of the country.

After all the information had been compiled, the product was test marketed in two Hispanic areas—Miami and San Antonio. The first step in delivering the product to the consumer was to create a sales kit to be distributed to the area retail store. This step would introduce the stores to the product in order to gain the shelf and floor space needed to market it successfully. The kit, in both English and Spanish, included a story about the product and its benefits, advertising and promotion support information, product spec sheets, radio advertisement scripts, television commercial storyboards, and point-of-purchase and case-card displays (in both Spanish and English). According to Davis, "In any marketing venture, it is important to get the retailer interested in your product."

The marketing campaign for the product involved television and radio advertisements and promotion. For the television advertisements there were two spots: one designed for adults, the second for children.

Television

The adult campaign integrated both animation and live action. The first part, approximately 15 seconds, was an animated segment highlighting the bear as spokesman for the product. The rest of the ad showed the preparation of the product, emphasizing the vitamin C ingredient and its nutritional benefits. These ads appeared on Spanish-language television in both target markets, placed during those hours that drew a significant female viewership (the targeted purchaser). The variation in these ads among Hispanic markets came with the musical jingles. Those in the Miami area had a salsa tempo, while a mariachi sound was used in San Antonio.

The child ads were somewhat different. They used only animation—the appeal less on the nutritional aspect of the product and more on the fun—again using the bear to entice the children to ask for the product. But instead of featuring them on Spanish-language television, the ads appeared during Saturday and Sunday morning cartoons on regular Anglo stations, in Spanish, without subtitles. According to Davis this was very important to the parents. "They felt that the company was interested in helping the Hispanic children maintain their Hispanic heritage." In addition, market research showed that this was the prime viewing time to catch Hispanic children, who, in general, are bilingual.

Radio

The radio ads for Delicioso used the t.v. ad jingle, with the same differentiation between markets. The music ran for 15 seconds at the beginning of the ad and again for 15 seconds at the end. In the center 30 seconds of the 60-second spot, a local personality—picked especially by the company to be appropriate for both the product and the community—provided live information on the product. The radio ads became an important part of Amstar's promotional advertising, as well as being used to announce special area appearances by the Delicioso bear.

Promotional Events

According to Davis, the real success of the campaign was due to its constant promotional aspect. With area visits by the bear in both target cities, along with store samplings and couponings, the product penetrated solidly into the Hispanic community.

The Bear

The real identity of the product focused on its spokesperson (or should we say "spokesbear"), "Delicioso," or "Oso." For the character, Adelante went to the company responsible for creating the Walt Disney character costumes and commissioned two costumes, one for each area, to be worn by a medium-build person.

"For the most part we hired college students, whose schedules would be flexible enough for them to attend daytime events throughout the area," Davis recalls. The bear was designed to be a macho bear, but one that was cute, yet not so cute as to be classified as effeminate. The bear traveled around the target markets to parks, ball parks, picnics, outdoor concerts, supermarkets, and local parades—anywhere that live, remote-broadcast coverage could be obtained.

One part of the promotional campaign that was used in local-area supermarkets featured the bear standing with a middle-aged Hispanic who worked as coordinator. The coordinator would take care of the sampling of the product, while the bear gave away coupons and bear buttons and entertained the shoppers.

In addition, the company sponsored theater parties where admission was based on presenting a proof-of-purchase coupon, and skating parties that were tied into the Carol Wright couponing program.

A Promotional Bonanza

The big seller. Due to error on the part of the packaging company (not Amstar, but a subcontracted packager), the second product shipment was delayed from August until the late fall. (The product is seasonal, with distribution in the spring and summer.) Needing to move the product quickly and get it off the shelves on time—without loss of product—Adelante created a special "Three Kings Day" promotion specifically for the Hispanic market. The campaign, geared toward mothers and grandmothers, appeared on local Spanish television and in local Spanish newspapers. The campaign said, "Make a child happy for the holidays. Fill out the coupon with the child's name and address, and enclose a proof-of-purchase coupon from Delicioso. With this order the child will receive a letter from the Delicioso bear—personally addressed—signed by the bear (paw print, of course)—telling the child why he or she should be proud to be Hispanic, and a story about the origin of Three Kings Day" (the 12th day of Christmas, January 6th, a holiday when the children receive their presents).

According to Davis the success was phenomenal, clearing out all the cases of Delicioso before the winter season began. In fact, it became the only Hispanic promotional campaign to win *Advertising Age's* "best regional/local marketing campaign" (1979).

Summing it Up

The campaign for Delicioso ran for two seasons, with an annual budget of a half-million dollars. In 1979, Amstar sold the product to a Latin market company, where the product is currently being sold. In a business where new-product failure is very high—Delicioso went beyond everyone's sales projections—and although it was marketed specifically for the Hispanic market, its appeal was beginning to cross over into the Anglo market. The product never went out of its test areas, "primarily," according to Davis, "because it was so successful there, the need to branch out had not yet arisen."

EASTERN AIRLINES: "THE WINGS OF THE AMERICAS"

Eastern Airlines, the popular East Coast carrier, has flown a highly successful campaign into the Hispanic market.

According to Gunther Saupe, Eastern's account management representative at Campbell-Ewald Latina, "When marketing Eastern's services to Hispanics, we needed to create a completely different campaign from the one our parent agency was using in the Anglo market."

In researching the Hispanic market for an air carrier, Campbell-Ewald Latina contracted Miami-based Strategy Research Corporation to conduct a series of person-to-person interviews in the top five Hispanic markets: New York, Miami, San Antonio, Chicago, and Los Angeles. SRC recorded 1,500 interviews on the reasons Hispanics fly, the most recent airline the individual used, recall on advertising campaigns, as well as which airline came to mind first.

The most important piece of marketing information came from the "why do you fly?" question. The research pointed to a different rationale for flying among Hispanics than among Anglos. "In the anglo market the primary reason for air travel is business, with discretionary travel coming in second," asserts Saupe. "But with Latin consumers, discretionary travel—that is, travel for the purpose of vacation or visiting friends and relatives—is their primary reason for flying. Business travel comes in second."

In addressing this desire for pleasure-oriented travel, Campbell-Ewald created a new theme line for the Hispanic consumer: "The wings of the Americas." According to Saupe, this tagline held a lot of identification for the Hispanic consumer. "In this statement we were conveying the breadth of

Eastern's coverage of the countries and cities in the Americas (North, Central, and South). For Hispanic travelers this was very important, since the majority of their preferred destinations are within these countries."

Eastern's flights in the Americas reach 140 cities in 25 countries. Most of these countries are Latin, and are destinations popular with Hispanic immigrants on the East Coast, primarily Puerto Ricans, and those immigrants from Central and South America. (Eastern is based in Miami, Florida, and flies to over 100 North American cities, in addition to servicing the Carribean and Latin America.) These consumers frequently travel back to their home countries for visits and vacations. The one exception is immigrants from Cuba—but their discretionary travel usually takes them to other Latin countries also covered by Eastern.

The Media

Eighty percent of Eastern's campaign to the Hispanic market is sent through the broadcast media, specifically television, and is highly targeted during the slow-season months. According to Saupe, "We target our campaign during the periods between March and June as well as September through November. This is not to say we do no promotion during the rest of the year, since we are constantly promoting Eastern's services, but research indicates these months to be the planning period for peak travel vacations. It is important for us to reach Hispanic consumers then in order to have their business later."

The radio and print media are used as support mechanisms for the campaigns featured on Hispanic television. Radio is used more often than print, but print plays an important part, particularly in advertising special fares and packages, where the complexities of the promotion need a larger frame.

The Campaign

The execution of Eastern's campaign to Hispanics has three parts. In using a three-step approach, the advertiser is introducing Eastern methodically to Hispanic consumers. As Saupe explains, the first part is what Eastern terms "brand equity."

"In the brand equity phase of advertising, the purpose is to develop Eastern's corporate image, to make the Hispanic consumer aware of its services and schedules..." and play up the solid background of the corporation. Among Hispanics, choices are often based on their perception of a company's strength.

This part of Eastern's campaign, according to Saupe, is generic. "Here, the emphasis is on image. We are appealing to all Hispanic consumers, and we make no differentiation among the segments of the Spanish-American community. This differentiation comes in our 'basic' and 'vacation oriented' campaigns."

"It is during the 'basic' section of the promotion," explains Saupe, "that we outline Eastern's specific destinations. The focus of these ads is the promotion of Latin countries where most of the immigrants in our U.S. ports are from. These ads promote the idea of visiting friends and relatives back in the homeland.

Successful Marketing to U.S. Hispanics & Asians

**Eastern offers you more of the Americas.
More than 140 cities, in 24 countries.**

EASTERN. THE WINGS OF THE AMERICAS.

Eastern Airlines advertising campaign for the Hispanic market, created by Campbell-Ewald Latina, Miami.

"This is one place where we include ethnic segmentation of the diverse Hispanic groups in terms of product promotion. Here, we promote specific Latin destinations in cities where the Hispanic population is composed of immigrants from that particular country. For example, in the New York metropolitan area we would use an Hispanic actor/model of Puerto Rican heritage, promoting flights to Puerto Rico," explains Saupe.

"Although most of our campaigns emphasize our low fares, this is not always possible." According to Saupe, "Due to fare regulations and restrictions in many of the Central and South American countries, fare promotion for international flights becomes something of no consequence. Because of this, our promotions to these countries center on our high-quality service and frequency of departure."

The third phase highlights vacation-oriented packages. Because of the nature of the community, this section of the campaign features many of the same destinations that are presented in the "basic" section. According to Saupe, "The locations in this section of the advertising are primarily international—Latin American countries. At many times these are the same destinations we are promoting in our basic line. The difference—here we highlight special vacation packages, like tours, rentals, and hotel packages. In addition we also promote domestic destinations, such as Disney World in Orlando, to consumers in New York and Chicago."

According to Saupe, "We realize that the Hispanic consumer has as wide an interest in travel as the general consumer. But we also realize that there is a difference, and we try to create our message to satisfy these needs."

The three-step strategy has been a success for Eastern and Campbell-Ewald Latina. In 1986, Eastern was the agency's largest account, with a budget of almost 10 million dollars. And it has paid off. Current research indicates that Eastern is No. 1 among Hispanics in top-of-mind awareness, in addition to being their airline of choice.

Not bad.

ALPO PET FOODS, INC.

What do you do if the competition is nipping at your feet in the Hispanic market? If you're a company like Alpo Pet Foods, Inc., you hire an experienced Hispanic agency to turn the situation around.

In 1984, Alpo noticed a trend in the Hispanic areas it had long dominated—the competition was gaining. For Alpo this seemed especially serious. For years, they had been unchallenged in the pet-foods industry. They needed to put a stop to the competition's gain, and (with luck) retrieve some of the percentage points they had lost.

Alpo called on Adelante Advertising, an Hispanic agency in New York City, to hold focus groups in the four top Hispanic markets: New York, Miami, Los Angeles, and San Antonio.

During these sessions, the questioning focused on the importance of the dog in the family environment—questions such as brand awareness (both of Alpo products and other dog-food products), general attitude toward dog-food preference, the type of dog Hispanics owned, the dog's value to the *family,* and general dog care.

The first point of importance from the marketing standpoint was that the purchaser of the product was more often than not the female head of household—in other words, Mom. She's the one who does the shopping for the pet and makes the product decisions.

It is also important to note that she does the shopping for the *family,* and the dog is considered a definite part of the Hispanic family. Her decisions about dog food and care are made as seriously as those made for other members of the family, with quality overriding price in the decision-making process. According to Davis, "What we found was that if the Hispanic consumer did not find her favorite dog food in her neighborhood store she would go somewhere else to make the purchase—very brand loyal and quality conscious."

Target Market

Alpo chose to target market their new Spanish-language campaign in two Hispanic ADIs, Miami and Los Angeles. According to Davis they chose these two areas out of the four on the basis of market share. "We found that in all the Hispanic markets, the areas where Alpo was losing the most of its share were Miami and Los Angeles. We felt that it was all-important, in terms of stopping this trend, to enter these markets as quickly as possible—and then proceed into the other areas."

The Media

When it came time to choose the media to reach the Hispanic market, Adelante suggested that Alpo use both television and radio. According to Davis, "Television and radio are very influential in the Hispanic market. In general the Hispanic consumer relies on these media for information. If the message they receive is *perceived* to be sincere, they will believe it as if it were gospel truth."

In general-market television spots, Alpo emphasizes the beef-chunk dinner from its product line. For the Anglo market this works well because Americans put a high value on beef and its nutritional benefits. In contrast, Hispanics favor a greater variety in their diet, placing as much preference on chicken and other food products—and less emphasis on beef. "And," emphasizes Davis, "if Hispanic consumers favor variety in their diets, they want the same benefit for their pets." To address this situation, the ads Adelante has produced for Alpo focus on the variety of flavors, as opposed to a single product.

Another difference between the Anglo and Hispanic campaigns is in the use of spokespersons. For the Anglo market, Lorne Greene presents the benefits of Alpo for a dog's nutrition. In the Hispanic campaign the use of a spokesperson has been dropped, favoring a number of different situations with a variety of products. The commercials are made more generic—to be distributed to all of the subgroups. To differentiate between markets, Adelante made cultural points in the musical backgrounds of the commercials.

The tagline for the ads ran, "Alpo, the food your dog deserves." According to Davis the message is that "If you care, you will give your pet the best." He adds, "It was important to remember the role that the dog plays in the Hispanic household: guardian, playmate, member of the family. The approach was, "You give your family the best, why not your dog?"

The success of the campaign was realized almost overnight—with the first SAMI reports showing increases in case movement. (SAMI—Selling Areas Marketing Inc.—provides status reports on warehouse withdrawal of product cases. The reports measure movement on the basis of previous year status, as well as comparison with competition.)

Before the first television season (13 weeks) had been completed, Alpo had stopped the trend favoring its competition in the Miami and Los Angeles areas. In addition it was beginning to gain back some of the market share it had lost. At present the campaign has been expanded into the Chicago area.

Promotion

There were, in addition, promotional events targeted to the Hispanic consumer. One unique program that Adelante set up for Alpo was turned in conjunction with veterinarians. According to Davis, "It was the first Spanish-language, professional relations program for the pet-foods industry."

What it involved was commissioning a retired Hispanic veterinarian to become an Alpo consultant. He would travel to veterinary conventions (where Alpo would take a booth) and visit animal hospitals, clinics, and vet offices in Hispanic neighborhoods. During these visits, the consultant would talk to the other veterinarians about their needs and their interests, as well as those of their clients. According to Davis, "This helped Alpo understand its consumers' needs in terms of pet nutrition and care—a line of communication that enabled Alpo to become an intrinsic part of the community."

J.C. PENNEY CO. INC.

Quinceañera. There's nothing quite like it in the Anglo-European tradition. Think of a sweet-16 party, then mix in elements of a bat mitzvah and a wedding, and the concept comes close. The celebrant has reached her fifteenth birthday—and it's her special day. She wears a princess dress, usually white, and is accompanied by 14 attendants and their escorts, all in tuxedos and gowns. There's a high mass, then a grand party, with a guest list swelling into the hundreds. A time for relatives and friends to honor a lovely girl. It's a tradition more often celebrated by U.S. Hispanics than by their relatives south of the border, the result of the simple fact of a higher standard of living.

It's also an excellent marketing opportunity for J.C. Penney, which has adapted many of its bridal salons to serve the guest of honor and her court—gowns, accessories, and services (silk flowers, photography and the like). Penney also includes *Quinceañera* gowns in its bridal fashion shows in Hispanic target markets, and the catalogs offer gowns specially and specifically identified for this event. A family may save for years for a daughter's *Quinceañera,* spending up to $10,000 or more on the event. The celebrant may spend $200 to $300 on the gown, and each of the attendants spends $100 to $170.

Although *Quinceañeras* are only one small part of the J.C. Penney approach to target marketing, the story exemplifies the firm's sensitive approach to Hispanic culture and family values. Most of the television spots, for example, use a story line dealing with Hispanic family life (with lots of children), and show four or five products during the scenario—a "soft sell" that puts the merchandise in a cultural context.

The story of J.C. Penney's interest in the Hispanic market begins in 1978, when Argentinian Patricia Asip, then the editor of the catalog division, wrote a memo underscoring the need for a close look at the Hispanic community. The memo was remembered a year later, when the firm planned to open some 250 catalog desks in California. Store and district managers, especially in the Los Angeles and Southern California areas, voiced a need for tools to reach the Spanish-speaking constituency.

The first tangible result: a 26-page brochure, written in Spanish, telling customers how to buy from the catalog. Coming before the 1980 census made the increase in Hispanic population a matter of headline news, the brochure was heralded by the *Wall Street Journal* and other publications as a pioneering effort by a major retailer. Demand for the shopping guide outgrew California, as requests poured in from areas such as Chicago and North Carolina (where there was a high concentration of migrant workers).

More important, the brochure "sensitized the company to a large and growing customer base," states Asip. The retailer responded by creating a new position, under the umbrella of corporate marketing and communication, with Asip at the helm as corporate Hispanic marketing programs manager. Asip feels that her position may be unique among U.S. retailers—a corporate-level "internal consultant" to all Hispanic marketing efforts nationwide.

Although the original idea of an Hispanic "shoppers' guide" is still in use, the format has streamlined into a much shorter (and slicker) brochure. Point of purchase is still a central area, however, and videos in Spanish help shoppers survey the merchandise. And, of course, there are newspaper inserts in Spanish to herald major merchandising events in the key markets.

But Asip talks with the greatest pride ("It's a labor of love," she says) about two other aspects of the Penney strategy: television spots and local Hispanic marketing teams.

A Coca-Cola or a McDonald's may be able to create one corporate spot and air it repeatedly. Not so with a retailer that stages some 22 merchandising events annually, each with a different blend of seasonal and personal wares. Each commercial has a life span of three days—and although the Spanish commercials may parallel their English-language counterparts, the selection of products may be different. And, of course, the spots are tailored to the audience, drawing again on all-important cultural traditions.

A 1986 Christmas spot, for example, depicts the Latin custom of Las Posadas, the procession symbolizing Mary and Joseph's journey to Bethlehem. The festivities include singing and the breaking of a *piñata,* which spews candy and toys for the children.

An earlier 1986 commercial, accenting various pieces of electronic equipment, drew its talent from "Que Pasa U.S.A.," a popular situation comedy. "*No hay que ser joven para ser moderno*"—"one need not be young to be modern"—is the message.

A 30-second spot with a story line underscoring family and traditional values may be awkward, Asip points out, but it can be done—and done well. Indeed, the idea of 22 separate commercials per year drives production costs up. The compensating factor: all production is done by in-house staff, an arrangement that also instills pride and enhances the idea that J.C. Penney is committed to the market, according to Asip.

Players in the Hispanic Arena

One of the most innovative ideas goes under the unassuming title "Local Hispanic Marketing Teams." Ten such teams now exist nationwide, in Chicago, Denver, and Miami, and at various locations in Arizona, North Carolina, and of course, California. Each team includes a district manager, a sales manager, and is chaired by a store manager.

Using a network approach, the team meets with Hispanic leaders in the area, both government and corporate. Luncheons provide an opportunity to talk about community events and corporate affairs—a sense of how Penney can enhance its role in the broader social life. The team gains a better understanding of how it can target special merchandise to Hispanic customers and how it can continue to enhance its services—bilingual personnel at the cataglog desks, for example.

Other Hispanic marketing team events: In Chicago when radio station WIND ("La Tremenda") celebrated its first anniversary, it used two stores (on two separate occasions) as the point of broadcast. Customers could come to the store to get free tickets, 50 at each broadcast, to a ball honoring the station's anniversary. It gave listeners a chance to come down and meet their favorite DJs, in addition to a chance to attend the party.

In Phoenix/Tucson, team members participated in the fifth annual Hispanic Women's Conference, an annual two-day event that provides leadership training, career guidance, and support for Hispanic women in the workplace.

In San Antonio, the store joined other sponsors to celebrate Fiestas Patrias, a lavish event featuring an array of ethnic foods, product information booths, and local and international entertainment. Penney stores sold admission tickets, and the company also benefited by having its name included on all advertising and t.v. and newspaper coverage.

And to keep its team members informed of what other teams are doing, J.C. Penney publishes *Noticias*—a newsletter especially for the company members working in the Hispanic market.

No discussion of Penney's approach would be complete without mention of the National Hispanic Corporate Council, a national *Fortune* 500 network of Hispanic corporate executives, established to exchange ideas, information, and research that will influence other corporations to focus on the Hispanic community. Asip serves as operations officer for the group, which is headed by Olga Aros, regional marketing manager with U.S.A. Today.

Add it all together and it's a comprehensive approach. How does one judge success? Simply by measuring the volume of merchandise that moves in the target areas, according to Asip. But isn't this an imprecise measurement? Isn't there a way of segmenting merchandise by Hispanic versus non-Hispanic purchase? "Not really," Asip says simply.

Parting note: the 1986 Junior Rose Bowl queen wore J.C. Penney *Quinceañera* gown stock 5969, and her attendants wore stock 228-5963, in baby blue.

NOT FOR ATTRIBUTION

Many of our respondents granted interviews on a not-for-attribution basis. Moreover, some of the respondents providing case study material placed limitations on the amount of detail we could publish—campaign budgets, for example. This section summarizes material gathered from those sources.

The Research Phase

Most respondents went to more than one source for their market research. Among other channels metioned:

- Use of company-compiled statistics on its current Hispanic consumer base; use of "tracking studies" to clarify current buying patterns.
- Identifying Hispanic individuals currently employed by the company; asking these individuals for input at various stages. Persons in distributorship or dealership positions proved especially valuable.
- Use of proprietary databases established by agencies with expertise in the market.
- Use of focus groups and face-to-face interviews to get an understanding of the Hispanic perception of the product at hand vis-a-vis the competitor's. Such research was usually conducted in a variety of urban centers, with an eye for regional variations.
- Use of joint industry research to define overall buying habits in, say, the top ten Hispanic markets.

In defining the national market, some respondents estimated the "uncounted" immigrant population to be about 5 million, bringing the total count to 24 million.

Virtually all respondents mentioned that they had drawn on material produced by Strategy Research Corporation. For some, the SRC work provided background on demographics, motivation, and purchasing power. For others, SRC served as a contracted agent for proprietary research.

Not all researchers felt a need to look at how the immigration/assimilation profiles are changing; those who did claim it was worth the effort. Respondents differ in the importance they place on segmentation within the Hispanic market. For a packaged food company, regional segmentation will be the most important ingredient for an upcoming campaign. For one durable goods manufacturer, the background music used in local television spots will provide the only segmentation. For a competitor, the segmentation will be complete: different local television commercials for each region.

Invariably, there was a need to convince corporate decision makers of the need to address the Hispanic market. The arguments often rested on these points:

- The company already had a significant Hispanic consumer base for its product or service.
- The Hispanic consumer is a higher-than-average user of the product or service.
- The Hispanic market is not always reachable by general advertising or marketing campaigns.
- Appealing to the Hispanic customer in Spanish would give the company an edge over its competition.

In amplification of the latter point, one respondent added that Spanish-language promotion played an important role in educating the Hispanic consumer in product evaluation and use. Obviously, more educated consumers will translate into higher sales for the company, the respondent feels.

Budgets

In most cases, between one and 10 percent of the marketing budget is targeted to Hispanics, although higher expenditures may be needed during a launch year. The longer a company has been in the market, the lower the percentage that goes to Hispanics. "If I told you how little I'm spending in the Hispanic market, you'd laugh at me," one soft-drink product manager told our researchers. The product in question has been in the Hispanic market for ten years, enjoying considerable success. Others have found that event promotion and direct dealer support are more efficient than conventional media. (See box, below.)

Enlisting the Retailers

The mid South may not be a thriving center of Hispanic population, but as headquarters for a home appliance manufacturing division, it's thoroughbred country for the development of retailer support.

A company spokesman estimates that one marketing dollar of every hundred goes into the Hispanic community. A further breakdown shows that while 30 percent of the expended funds go to advertising, a far more massive 64 percent is dedicated to "merchandising"—efforts to supply retailers with in-store and locally placed promotional materials. The marketing logic is unmistakably clear: Dealers operating in Hispanic communities sell the product to Hispanic customers; the dealers need the support.

The second-language program has a long history. "We've been doing it for about a thousand years," jokes the spokesman, "and it holds a steady portion of our overall marketing budget." Expansion may come soon. "There are markets where the Hispanic population is becoming integrated, and in other areas there's a blurring of the border between the U.S. and Mexico. I think it's just a matter of time until we have Hispanic governors. In the long term, socially and commercially, it may be more realistic to talk about a North American market rather than a U.S. market."

Three parts of the respondent's organization are involved in the second-language effort: the field sales organization, which includes bilingual representatives; the toll-free 800-number operation where 15 of the 250 employees speak Spanish; and at the manufacturing center headquarters, which includes a small number of Hispanics among its 178 managers and employees.

"Spanish-language marketing modules originate at the manufacturing headquarters. The corporate headquarters (at another location) does some Hispanic media buying, between $300,000 and $400,000 worth of Hispanic radio time in 1986. But outside of huge markets like New York, Los Angeles and Miami, the company counts on local retailers to buy space or time in local media."

The company provides sales literature, point-of-purchase material, and product information sheets in Spanish, as well as ad copy. Retailers use these tools and make local buys.

"Throughout the calendar year we have retail promotions which many of our dealers take over as their own," notes the spokesman. "Rebate programs, national sales days with banners, summertime deals on refrigerator ice makers . . . on the West Coast we do an annual truckload sale. Though it's tough to measure the success of these specific programs, over the long haul we like the results."

But success in the Hispanic market has not yet spurred the company to action in Asian languages. "I don't really see that as being a large segment of our business. Some producers have a greater incentive to segment the hell out of the population—products where it's typical to have a hundred-million dollar national advertising budget. With that amount, you can segment to the Vietnamese, Koreans—everybody."

"But when you chop it up into too many pieces, you have production costs becoming more and more of the total, and you don't sell anything with production costs; you sell with advertising. So in terms of production as well as media buys, it's TV no, newspapers yes for the second-language markets. Newspapers are the most economical buy."

Like other respondents in this category, the company will wait until an Asian-language market segment grows to 10 or 15 percent of the whole population, rivaling today's Hispanic segment in terms of percentage."

Some of the players do, however, follow a "10 percent" rule (since about one in ten Americans is of Hispanic origin). This is certainly true for one of our respondents in the consumer products area (1986 sales in excess of $1.5 billion). Ten percent of the $37 million marketing budget is allocated to target Hispanics. Of this budget, about 40 percent goes for advertising, 35 percent for publicity and promotion, 15 percent for public and community relations.

Another respondent, a local service company operating in a dense Hispanic population area, plans to double its current Hispanic budget for the year ahead (20 percent, rather than 10). Much of the additional budget will go to establish a bilingual service capability. The respondent hopes that this tactic will result in increased purchases of add-on services.

Another respondent (a national company) underscored the importance of bilingual service as he talked about the company's new Hispanic 800-number service. "Our research found that a number of our consumers are Spanish dependent. When they call us, it is usually to get answers to questions or solutions to problems, and the best way to assist them is to have someone on duty who can speak to them in their own language. In addition, we provide collateral information on our services and products, translated into Spanish. It's important to us that we understand what's important to our customers—and to put forward a concerted attempt to address their needs." Competition for the service in question is currently fierce, and the respondent believes that the bilingual capability will translate into consumer loyalty.

Promotion

Respondents differ considerably on which media provide the best payback. On one point, however, there is an unshakable consensus: public relations is the cornerstone of a successful campaign.

Players in the Hispanic Arena

Being a good corporate citizen—the idea is playing on Madison Avenue now more than ever before. For the Anglo market, such initiatives are seen as one way of promoting American-made products in the face of increasing foreign competition. For the Hispanic market there is an added importance: attracting new customers who have previously been ignored by corporate America.

One durable goods manufacturer is currently talking about forgoing its emphasis on product and concentrating heavily on corporate image in the Hispanic community. Radio and print campaigns will emphasize the corporation's work in support of minority dealerships, banking concerns, college endowment programs, and the like. The radio campaign will use an Hispanic celebrity to present the message lyrically. The print campaign will put the spotlight on an Hispanic distributor, who intertwines his personal story with information about how the company has helped Hispanics.

Print and radio will carry the image campaign nationally; local television will segment the market and sell the products. Another respondent reverses the media roles, using local television for information on community work, print for the sell copy.

Other respondents talked about their work with LULAC and La Raza, specific festivals, fairs, leadership conferences, and the like.

One respondent sees such involvement as integral for what he calls a "stimulatory and constant" campaign. "The market has to be constant, because the community is constantly evolving, and it is important for us to be continually emphasizing our message. There is a continuous stream of new Hispanic immigrants into the United States, and we want to be their company of choice.

"Our message to the community must also be stimulatory, because once we've got their business we cannot assume that they are going to stay with us. The problem with the Hispanic market is that, after a while, they begin to mainstream. And with this assimilation they start to shop around for services, just like the Anglo market. What we have to do is keep them with us."

The latter respondent is one of serveral major players currently putting a similar approach in place for the Asian community.

4

Hispanic Media

HISPANIC PRINT has its problems. Lack of centralization is a major one. Everyone protests that too little attention is paid to Hispanic print, that Madison Avenue is passing by the written word for more efficient television and radio segments. Why? It is simply easier to place ads in the electronic media because of the existing networks. In addition, radio and television reach an enormous number of consumers in diverse locations. As yet, this is not possible in print.

According to *Hispanic Business*, in 1986 only 8.3 percent of the total advertising expenditure in the Hispanic market was allocated to print. In fact the only media receiving a lesser percentage were outdoor (3 percent) and transit (0.9 percent) ads. (See Exhibit 4.1.)

But this is not print's only problem. It is time for the industry do some reflection on its situation. It needs to develop its circulation and research information in order to make its space more appealing.

Says Felix Guttierez, a professor of journalism at the University of Southern California: "There are really only three cities that offer daily opportunities in the Hispanic print media: New York, Los Angeles, and Miami. For the most part, the papers are small, and in some cases their circulation and schedule figures are unmonitored. This creates a big question mark in the minds of those placing advertisements, who have no way of knowing who is receiving their message."

Guttierez prescribes a three-step process to improve the position of the print medium. "Auditing is an important first step in bringing in advertising revenue. If you have the numbers, show them. This is what is going to convince the marketers of your value.

Hispanic Media

Exhibit 4.1. Advertising expenditure in the Hispanic media, 1986.

National television (Univision): $64 million

National radio: $46.8 million

Local television (Univision affiliates): $78 million

Local radio: $83.2 million

Independent television (national and local, excluding Univision): $42.3 million (*Note:* This is the largest increase in the market.)

Print: $33.2 million

Outdoor: $12 million

Promotion: $3.5 million

Transit: $3.5 million

Total advertising expenditure in 1986: $398 million

Source: *Hispanic Business*

The expenditure in print, which is 8.3 percent of the total advertising expenditure, is actually lower than it was in 1985 (9.9 percent). According to *Hispanic Business* there was actually a decrease, or in the best cases, a stabilization between the percentage splits in advertising revenue. The other medium that shows an increase was the independent television group, which increased by 4.5 percent (from 6.1 to 10.6). Exhibit 4.2 (page 46) shows the major Hispanic publications with relevant cost data.

"Second, the print industry needs to *work together*. This is all for the good of the industry. There is little competition between papers in Los Angeles and those in New York. By using a network similar to the networks in the television and radio industries, ad placement can be made simply through one contact, with showcases in multiple cities.

"Third, the print media needs to be more aggressive in gaining circulation. Newsstand sales just don't create the kinds of numbers marketers are looking for. Subscription sales do."

This is how Stephen Beale, senior editor for *Hispanic Business*, perceives the problem: "The most common complaint we hear from the agencies is that there is a lack of research on the market—that the figures lack reliability and that there is no conclusive information on the consumer base for the higher priced products. To get these advertisers, more research will have to be conducted by each of the publications. More important, those studies have to be in-depth profiles of their readers, in order to convince advertisers that the consumer is ready and willing to pay for their products."

AUDITING

A significant problem within the Hispanic print industry is the lack of voluntary auditing by its members. According to Kader Afif, president of Advertising Information Monitoring (AIM), a print monitoring service in New York City, "The figures from the media itself, in terms of circulation, are for the most part unreliable." This assertion is echoed again and again by those in the industry, and most strongly by those publications which have already completed the auditing procedure.

Why is auditing so important? Peter Bellas, advertising director for *La Opinion*, the Spanish-language daily in Los Angeles, contends that "The advertising community lives and dies with the numbers. Without audited figures giving a definite idea of how many people they are reaching, advertisers are very wary about committing their budgets. The rating services are becoming a highly important element in the industry."

Bellas adds, "Agencies will pay more attention to those publications that can back up their numbers."

Arnaldo Jimenez, marketing director for De Armas publications in New York, sees it this way: "Because of the lack of credibility in the media, auditing is becoming a very important feature in the print industry. We have signed up with ABC (the Audit Bureau of Circulation) and expect the figures to be in during the summer of '87. The auditing procedure will greatly benefit those who have complied, because agencies and marketing managers will be more likely to go with the publications that can verify their numbers."

But, according to John Kriete, national advertising manager for *El Diario/La Prensa* in New York, auditing is not the central focus. "Auditing is not going to change the industry and make it more popular," stated Kriete in a June 1987 interview. "What is needed is something along the lines of a national paper or a network among the pre-existing papers. Creating a better channel of information among the Hispanic communities will promote better publications, as well as providing advertisers with a simpler means of placing ads across the country. These two processes will in turn bring in revenue as a result of higher circulation figures and increased advertising spending."

Kriete is not the only one who believes that networking is the way to go. Both Bellas and Guttierez see the move into a national frame as benefiting the print industry, in the same way it has benefited the broadcast channels.

"In the Anglo media, as well as in the Hispanic broadcast media, there is the ability to buy nationally. As yet, this is not available in the Hispanic print media, and for growth this will have to change," contends Bellas. Guttierez adds further emphasis: "To a large extent, print is locally owned and managed, independent of all other sources. Because of this individuality, placement becomes one here, one there, one somewhere else. There needs to be a link. Something that makes it easier."

WHAT DO YOU MEAN THERE'S NO HISPANIC PRINT NETWORK—
WHAT ABOUT NAHP, INC.?

At the close of work July 1, 1987, the response from our experts in the Hispanic print media was that the biggest gap in the industry was the inability to make a national buy.

But during the month of July all that changed. The NAHP, Inc. was formed.

A spin-off of the non-profit National Association of Hispanic Publications, created in 1982, the **NAHP, Inc.**, a for-profit organization, is attempting to do what its parent could not—create a single source where advertising agencies can send one insertion order, write out one check, and place their ad in up to 50 different publications, nationwide.

The president of the new organization is Zeke Montes, publisher of *Teleguia*, a television guide publication in the Chicago area. According to Montes, the ability to make a national buy was previously available through the NAHP as of 1985, with their rep company, Entrada, and its agent Bruce Kaplan. But the response was minimal, at best. "It appeared that the agencies were not interested in working with a rep, but wanted more direct contact with those involved in the publications. This prompted the formation of the NAHP, Inc.

"Essentially, the NAHP, Inc. is a group of Hispanic print publishers from the New York, Chicago, and Los Angeles areas, representing approximately 50 publications nationwide. Our list includes all of the daily Spanish-language newspapers, most of the weeklies, and a good proportion of the magazines (primarily Spanish t.v. publications). So far the response has been positive."

That positive response is coming from three areas, two of which have either commited money, to the sum of $40,000, or are close to signing a contract for approximately $600,000 in advertising revenue.

Montes sees the job of the NAHP, Inc. as "working to better develop the Hispanic identity in the print industry. Our biggest obstacle is creating credibility for our member publications. To do this, we must get all those who have not yet verified their circulation by audit to do so. Our goal is to have all publications audited by the end of 1988, using advertising dollars as the incentive."

"Besides the auditing procedure, we have to get recognition. One initial step we are taking is a seminar we are holding in Chicago this August. Although the primary goal of this particular meeting is to influence the regional buy for Chicago's Hispanic publications, we will also be discussing the potential of national buys. In addition, we are looking to set up similar seminars in other cities, such as New York and Los Angeles, with the same aim."

BROADCAST, THE ENEMY OF THE PRINT INDUSTRY?

Is broadcast really the print industry's enemy, or is it just that broadcasters have been around a lot longer, and are better at pursuing the advertisers to buy their time? According to Guttierez, "The broadcast market is more aggressive and adept at understanding Madison Avenue and has what it takes to get the marketers interested in its ventures."

On the other side, Bellas gives it a more amorous complexion. "The advertising agencies have fallen in love with television and radio, not only in the Hispanic market, but in the general market as well. Advertising expenditures for the broadcast media and the print medium are on the same level in the Hispanic market as in the Anglo market."

But Jimenez perceives it in terms of revenue. "It is a lack of understanding on the part of the agencies and marketers as to the benefits of the print medium. The agencies' buy decisions are influenced by the revenues that can be generated by the broadcast media as opposed to the print segment."

Finally, there is the point of literacy. The most damaging complaint about the Hispanic community is the perception of Hispanics as illiterate laborers. Is illiteracy really a specific problem in the Hispanic community? For the most part, our experts suggest that it is not. Dr. Carlos Arce, president of Nu Stats, a marketing research firm in Austin, Texas, says "In terms of the amount of time spent reading among Hispanics, the distribution of the very well read and the unread is about the same as in the general population."

"The broadcast media are oversold in the Hispanic community," contends Guttierez. "Sure, there is a correlation between education and income, which can point to a lower readership level among Hispanics. But reading newspapers is part of their culture. This is not going to change because they are north of the border. In Latin American countries there is a plentitude of print channels. In fact, there are more daily newspapers in Tiajuana then there are in San Diego."

Guttierez suggests that "marketers should look carefully at the audience data in the areas where the Hispanic population is substantial. They will find strong readership patterns among the Latino population, making the print industry look very strong."

THE PRINT VEHICLE: WHAT IT OFFERS

According to our sources, the points that make print viable for marketers have to do with its abiltiy to deliver and reinforce a message over a longer period of time. Because of reader loyalty, print provides credibility. But most important, the growth of the Spanish-language print industry will be most affected by immigration patterns. Continued immigration from Latin American countries will provide the reasons for advertising in Spanish-language media.

"Immigration patterns are going to be a large determining factor in the Hispanic print industry," Guttierez believes. "If immigration remains stable, these new arrivals will be looking for information in their own language, and the print industry will boom."

"But it is not only the Spanish-language print industry that has to take notice. Along with continued immigration, there is a rising assimilation pattern as well," contends Guttierez. "The English print medium has to take notice of the Hispanic population, and gear its message to them. With continued assimilation, the Hispanic immigrant will begin to look at a wider scope of information sources. If these publications are ready, they will serve a rising Hispanic consumer class. If not, the loss could be dramatic, especially in areas Hispanics dominate."

According to Arce, "The real growth in the Hispanic print medium is due to the influx of Latin American publications into the United States. This has occurred because of immigration from Central and South America, and the immigrants' need for Spanish-language print."

Jimenez repeats the message: "Marketers do not realize that the print message can reinforce their broadcast message. Commercials placed on television and radio are easily forgotten or mixed up. With the print medium, the ads are more available and accessible for review. They can also provide essential reminders of the messages heard in broadcast."

According to Kriete, "Because of the limited number of newspapers with which the U.S. Hispanic market is covered—only seven Spanish-language dailies in the country—it is not hard to understand why print receives a lower percentage of the advertising budget. But print has an advantage over the other media that must be exploited: its lasting credibility. Hispanics in general are very loyal to their papers and value their point of view, as well as the advertisers who support them."

To some, the future looks bright. According to Randy Schmidt, vice president/advertising of *El Sol de Texas*, a Spanish-language weekly in the Dallas/Fort Worth area, "the Hispanic print industry has a very bright future in the United States, but it is up to those of us involved in the industry to make advertisers and marketers aware of our importance. Our biggest selling advantage is the fact that a newspaper's life is longer than that of a 30-second commercial. In the television and radio industries, the commercials may intrigue but can be easily forgotten. In print, the ad stays around for a longer time. This is our advantage. For advertisers, their best impact on the community would be a combined effort, selling on television and radio to attract interest and then following up in print as a reinforcement."

Bellas sees the growth of the industry this way: "The Spanish-language print industry will grow. Right now there is a lot of confusion in the market, due to conflicting trends. Of course, the Hispanic population is assimilating. But there is also a trend in advertising toward presenting the message in Spanish. In addition there is a movement by significant money players, such as Hallmark, into the market—committing dollars to the Spanish-language channels.

"Yet, there is a growing movement toward making the United States a single-language country—as seen in the recent ballot in Calfornia decreeing English as the state's official language. So, the area is cloudy, but the direction toward second-language media looks favorable, most importantly because of the revenue sources coming from Hispanic avenues."

WHAT MAKES PRINT TICK

A review of media information from the Hispanic print industry and data compiled by outside sources has yielded important insights into the medium. One publication that presents a focus on the industry is *Hispanic Media, U.S.A.*, a narrative guide to the entire Hispanic media, published by the Media Institute in 1987. It provides information on a number of publications, in addition to covering television and radio stations targeting Hispanics.

The guide makes eight points with regard to the Hispanic print industry:

- Consumers of Hispanic print tend to be more bilingual than those who tune into television and radio broadcasts.
- Advertising in Hispanic newspapers tends to be local, with national advertising increasing—all magazine advertising is national.
- The newspapers' focus is more on Hispanic-American news and is more neighborhood-oriented.
- The international focus tends to be on news from Hispanic countries, specified to the area—Mexico and Central and South America.
- The news is predominately from wire services and press releases, because of small news staffs. Staff reporters are usually used to cover local events; international news is covered from the outside.

- Most papers translate ads from English to Spanish.
- On the whole, readers of Hispanic print are better educated than the Hispanics in the community at large.
- Hispanic publications that have transformed their editorial content to English have done so because it is the language of business and assimilation. They target the upwardly mobile Hispanic consumer, who prefers to read in English but still has a strong commitment to his or her Hispanic heritage and things that are predominately Hispanic.

CLOSE-UP ON HISPANIC PRINT

Next, a look at some of the major Hispanic print avenues. Exhibit 4.2 provides circulation and rate data for selected publications; the text that follows fills out the picture.

Exhibit 4.2. Major Hispanic publications and advertising costs.

Publication		1 page	½ page	¼ page
Hispanic Business Circulation: 110,000 (audited)		$ 4,375	$ 3,110	$ 1,840
Vista Circulation: 1,000,000 (audited)	b&w 2 color 4 color	$21,900 $24,000 $27,000	$11,800 $12,700 $15,100	$ 9,300 $10,800 $12,900
	back cover: $33,700;		inside cover: $29,000	
Selecciones Circulation: 130,000 (audited)	b&w 2 color 4 color	$ 2,285 $ 2,590 $ 3,110	$ 1,475 $ 1,690 $ 2,020	
La Voz de Houston Circulation: 40,000		$ 1,150	$ 600	$ 320
Noticias de Mundo Circulation: 25,000 (audited)		$1,788	$ 934	$ 510
El Herald Circulation: 74,351		$3,698	$1,969	$1,005
Diario Las Americas Circulation: 64,093		$1,540	$ 770	$ 385
El Diario/La Prensa Circulation: 60,000		$2,025	$1,012	$ 446

Hispanic Media

El Sol de Texas Circulation: 20,000			$1,260	$ 630	$ 315
La Opinion (local display rates) Circulation: 68,089 (audited)			$1,323	$ 661	$ 330

THE DE ARMAS NETWORK*			1 page	½ page	inside/back
Vanidades		b&w	$2,200	$1,375	
Circulation: 70,320		2-color	$2,700	$1,720	
		4-color	$3,300	$2,065	$3,795/$4,125
Cosmopolitan en Espanol		b&w	$1,700	$1,065	
Circulation: 51,915		2-color	$2,125	$1,330	
		4-color	$2,550	$1,595	$2,935/$3,190
Buenhogar		b&w	$1,200	$ 750	
Circulation: 25,390		2-color	$1,500	$ 940	
		4-color	$1,800	$1,125	$2,070/$2,250
Tu		b&w	$1,150	$ 720	
Circulation: 17,500		2-color	$1,440	$ 900	
		4-color	$1,725	$1,080	$1,985/$2,155
Harper's Bazaar En Espanol		b&w	$ 780	$ 490	
Circulation: 7,650 (audited)		2 color	$ 975	$ 610	
		4 color	$1,170	$ 730	$1,345/$1,465
Ideas Para Su Hogar		b&w	$ 720	$ 450	
Circulation: 10,050		2 color	$ 900	$ 565	
		4 color	$1,080	$ 675	$1,240/$1,350
Ritmo		b&w	$ 700	$ 440	
Circulation: 10,850		2 color	$ 875	$ 545	
		4 color	$1,050	$ 655	$1,210/$1,315
TV Y Novelas		b&w	$1,130	$ 705	
Circulation: 56,500		2 color	$1,415	$ 885	
		4 color	$1,695	$1,060	$1,950/$2,120

THE DE ARMAS NETWORK* (continued)		1 page	½ page	inside/back
Mecanica Popular				
	b&w	$1,010	$ 630	
Circulation: 6,650	2 color	$1,265	$ 790	
	4 color	$1,515	$ 945	$1,740/$1,895
Hombre				
	b&w	$1,200	$ 750	
Circulation: 9,450	2 color	$1,500	$ 940	
	4 color	$1,800	$1,125	$2,079/$2,250
Geomundo				
	b&w	$1,170	$ 730	
Circulation: 13,700	2 color	$1,465	$ 915	
	4 color	$1,755	$1,095	$2,020/$2,195
Padres y Hijas	b&w	$ 930	$ 580	
	2 color	$ 1,165	$ 730	
Circulation: 10,000	4 color	$ 1,395	$ 870	$1,600/$1,745
Muy Interesante	b&w	$ 830	$ 520	
Circulation: NA	2 color	$ 1,040	$ 650	
	4 color	$ 1,245	$ 780	$1,430/$1555

*Added discount for multibuy within the network. Also regionally split among Miami, New York/New Jersey, California/Texas.

Vista

Vista's pitch to the advertising community is spelled out right on its media-kit cover:

At last. A print medium that reaches Hispanics by the millions!

> It's National
> It's a Magazine
> It's Targeted
> It's Verifiable
> It's Effective
> It's Efficient
> It's Quality
> It's Vista

Vista magazine reaches the Hispanic community during the first week of every month as a supplement in local-area newspapers. Launched in September 1985, with a distribution network of 12 newspapers and a circulation totaling 427,000, it has grown within two years to 25 papers, with a guaranteed circulation of one million.

Written in English, *Vista* envisions itself as a "communications link" among the various Hispanic communities in the United States. The specific target audience is the young, upwardly mobile, well-educated, bilingual Hispanic. Essentially, it is a market that is forgotten by both Anglo and Spanish-language media.

Before the launch, *Vista* commissioned a market study by Strategy Research Corporation in 11 cities. The results pointed to a high preference for a magazine written in English but designed and edited for Hispanic sensibilities.

The original research proved valid, according to a study conducted five months into the distribution launch. The study presents a positive reaction to *Vista's* editorial content and confirms the premises on which *Vista* was established. It was performed by Research Resources in Westlake Village, California. The data on the test is available in *Vista's* media kit. The basic findings were:

1. Overwhelming acceptance and very high interest in the publication.
2. Initial loyalty and emotional bonding with its readers.
3. Endorsement of current format and editorial content as addressing the needs, tastes, and interests of its readers.

Vista has its greatest popularity in the Southwest portion of the United States, where Hispanics tend to be third- and fourth-generation Americans. The only large Hispanic center *Vista* has yet to penetrate is the New York metropolitan area. *Vista* is currently negotiating for distribution there, which, if successful, will boost it from a monthly to a weekly publication.

De Armas Publications: Hispanic Magazine Network, U.S.A.

International in scope, the Hispanic magazine network consists of 13 publications. Its initial distribution was in Latin America, but it has pushed circulation into the United States, following increased immigration. For advertising purposes there are four buy positions, one for the total U.S. circulation and three in specific Hispanic target areas: New York/New Jersey, Miami, and California/Texas.

Moving toward a subscription base, the network is currently 40 percent home-subscription and 60 percent newsstand sales. According to Arnaldo Jimenez, marketing director for De Armas, the firm hopes to increase home subscription to 55 or 60 percent by 1988. Auditing for the publications should be completed by summer 1987.

In 1984, De Armas contracted Monroe Mendelsohn Research to conduct a readership study of its subscribers, including information on types of products and services bought, used, and consumed. Complete research information is available in the De Armas media kit.

Special supplements are available during the year in specific publications. For example, a medical health guide in *Hombre De Mundo*; a summer shopping supplement in *Vandidades, Cosmopolitan, Harper's,* and *Buenhogar*; a holiday-season supplement in *Vanidades, Buenhogar, Cosmo,* and *Harper's*; and a home-decoration supplement in *Vandidades, Cosmo, Harper's, Buenhogar,* and *Ideas Para Su Hogar*.

In addition, special-interest annuals are put out by *Vanidades, Buenhogar, Ideas, Mecanica Popular, Tu,* and *Hombre de Mundo* on topics of reader interest. Advertisers are encouraged to take advantage of the annuals, which are newsstand-distributed along with the magazines. Only full-page ads are available in the annuals.

Although it is currently not audited, De Armas contracted with the ABC auditing service in early 1987 and expects to have an audit report by summer 1987. Also, De Armas has contracted with Strategy Research Corporation to update its readership survey, with information on its big markets: where they are, who is there, what they earn, what they buy, brand preferences, and the decisions behind readers' choices. This, De Armas feels, will help advertisers advance their strategies and make correct placements within the network.

The publications are:

1. *Vanidades*. Established in 1961—biweekly. A women's magazine focusing on fashion, beauty, food, and home decoration. Median age: 29.5. The most popular magazine in the collection. Internationally known.
2. *Cosmopolitan en Espanol*. Established in 1973—monthly. A women's magazine, conceived in the mold of its Anglo predesessor, but with a decidedly Hispanic flavor. Median age: 28.6.
3. *Buenhogar*. Established in 1967—biweekly. Created for the modern, well educated, affluent married woman. Median age: 31.5.
4. *Harper's Bazaar en Espanol*. Established in 1980—monthly. Editorial content is similar to its Anglo counterpart but edited with the Hispanic woman in mind. Median age: 30.2.
5. *Tu*. Established in 1981—monthly. A magazine for the young woman, on fashion, beauty, and entertainment. Median age: 19.5.
6. *Ideas Para Su Hogar*. Established in 1978—monthly. A service magazine, featuring tips on cooking, decorating, gardening, sewing. Median age: 29.7.
7. *TV Y Novelas*. Established 1982—biweekly. Covers television programming, with editorials on t.v. and film personalities, especially those involved in the novelas. Median age: 33.8.
8. *Ritmo*. Established in 1982—biweekly. A music-industry magazine, for the young person. Median age: 29.3.
9. *Geomundo*. Established in 1977—monthly. A geographic magazine, featuring articles and pictorials on exotic regions of the world. Median age: 34.4.
10. *Hombre de Mundo*. Established in 1976—monthly. A men's magazine, featuring editorials on world economy, business, politics, travel, fashion, the arts, and sports. Median age: 31.5.
11. *Mecanica Popular*. Established in 1947—monthly. The Spanish version of *Popular Mechanics*, covering automobiles, electronics, science, photography, audio and video equipment, and workshop projects. Median age: 31.7.
12. *Padres y Hijos*. Established 1987—monthly. A magazine devoted to parents, with editorials on marriage, sexuality, pregnancy, and family. Median age: NA.
13. *Muy Interesante*. Established 1987—monthly. A magazine dedicated to the sciences. Median age: NA.

Diario Las Americas

Founded in 1953, *Diario Las Americas* is the twelfth largest daily newspaper in Florida, serving the Miami area. Two-thirds of its distribution is through home delivery.

A general-interest, family-oriented publication, *Diario* carries complete coverage of international, national, state, and local news as well as sports, finance, food, lifestyle, travel, and other feature sections.

Strategy Research performed a reader-profile study in 1985. The researchers conducted face-to-face interviews with 410 subscribers. These participants were randomly selected from housewives or heads of households. An interesting finding: 88 percent of the subscribers are of Cuban descent.

Diario's media kit also includes a market study on the Miami area, highlighting population distribution, ethnic background, growth, education, and purchasing power. The brochure also contains general information on the paper's editorial focus: international and national news; news from Latin America and Spain; local and state news; sports, economy and finance; a business-world section four times a week; and entertainment. There are also yearly special sections for Cuban Independence Day, the Latin Chamber of Commerce, and 10 de Octobre.

Hispanic Business

"The magazine for growth companies and ladder-oriented professionals," boasts the masthead of *Hispanic Business*. Established in 1979, this monthly publication is targeted for the English-dominant Hispanic business person.

Hispanic Business is the most widely quoted Hispanic business publication source in the industry. With an extensive database on the U.S.-Hispanic business economy and the Hispanic professional segment, and on the consumers comprising that market, *Hispanic Business* presents an all-encompassing look at the Hispanic business community. Editorial emphasis is on information organized and presented for practical use.

Hispanic Business reaches one of the fastest growing affluent segments of the U.S. population—the middle- and upper-class Hispanic man and woman. Research indicates that its consumers have achieved some level of college education (83.2 percent), are now in their prime purchasing years (median age: 41), and earn a personal income of $37,580 per year.

The readership study was conducted by Scarborough Research Corporation in 1985. Using mail questionnaires sent to randomly chosen subscribers, Scarborough received a return of 327 forms out of a total of 1,000 mailed.

In addition to its subscription and newsstand circulation, *Hispanic Business* is distributed to 100 college and university placement offices around the country.

Topics covered in 1987 include:

- Managing your finances/taxes
- Jobs and careers
- Franchising
- The leading CEOs
- Venture capital

- The *Hispanic Business* 500
- Show business
- 100 influentials
- Entrepreneurial professionals
- High tech
- The 100 fastest growing companies
- The Hispanic market

We asked Stephen Beale, senior editor for *Hispanic Business*, why the text is printed in English. "It is our feeling that English is the international language of business," he answered. "Most Hispanics speak and read English as well as—sometimes better than—Spanish. Particularly our readership. They tend to be in higher income levels than the general Hispanic population, well educated, and either very well assimilated into American culture or at least moving in that direction."

According to a Price-Waterhouse study conducted in 1985, *Hispanic Business* was the second most read source of information on the Hispanic community by Hispanic business people. (No. 1 was their own local newspaper.) All of the reading sources listed were English-language publications.

La Opinion

A family owned publication, *La Opinion* was founded by Ignacio E. Lozano in 1926 and is currently under the direction of his grandson, Jose I. Lozano.

A general-interest newspaper featuring news, entertainment, commentary, business, and sports, *La Opinion* also carries a special Thursday edition called "Los Vecinos," reaching 200,000 households in the Los Angeles area. Hand-delivered, Los Vecinos features a blend of communtiy news, fashion, and entertainment.

Los Angeles issues are the guiding focus of the paper, but national and international news, especially from Central and South America, are featured daily.

Included in *La Opinion's* media kit are demographic and psychographic statistics regarding the Los Angeles Hispanic market, as well as a readership study conducted in 1985 by Scarborough Research Corporation.

According to Peter Bellas, advertising director: "Our paper is targeted toward the Hispanic community, which we feel is a very well-defined audience. They are not readers of the *L.A. Times*. In fact, *La Opinion* is their major source of information on both the LA community and the world in general. Our audience reads and thinks in Spanish, an audience that no other paper in the area is reaching."

La Voz De Houston

A weekly paper servicing the Houston area, *La Voz* is the brainchild of Olga Ordonez, a Cuban immigrant who came to the United States in 1962. *La Voz* provides the Hispanic community with a format that presents an exchange of ideas within the Hispanic world. It brings the community news from throughout the United States, Mexico, Latin America, and the world, as well as local and state news, sports, entertainment, social events, features, editorials, and more.

La Voz contains a special magazine-style insert, written in a lighter vein than the general newspaper. Entertainment, social events, and women's features are covered in this section. *La Voz* also features a section in English called "Community," geared toward providing news, features and columns of particular interest to Mexican-Americans.

Houston has the fifth-largest Hispanic population in the United States, and *La Voz* pursues coverage of Hispanic interest not available in the traditional American media. *La Voz* has a vast readership among Hispanic professionals—doctors, lawyers, engineers, professors, and is used as text material for Spanish classes at Rice University, the University of Houston, and the University of St. Thomas.

La Voz considers itself a uniting force for the Hispanic population, a voice for the community.

Selecciones

"Speak in Spanish! And reach the $60-billion Hispanic market."

So reads the pitch for *Selecciones,* the Spanish-language edition of *Reader's Digest*, which has been targeting Hispanic-America since 1971. Prior to U.S. distribution, the publication was available only in Latin America.

According to its media kit, *Selecciones* readers are at a higher economic and achievement level than average Hispanic consumers. They are mature, well educated, management-level executives with higher-than-average incomes, larger families, and more stable lifestyles. The biggest selling point is reader loyalty: 70 percent of the circulation is by subscription.

Advertising in *Selecciones* can be done in conjunction with ads placed in the Anglo edition—for further discount rates.

Included in the media kit is a demographic profile of the readers, conducted by Starch Inra Hooper, Inc., in July 1984. The survey was conducted with a mailed questionnaire; 971 questionnaires were sent and 430 returned.

The marketing information indicates that Hispanic-Americans are proud of their traditions and concerned with preserving their identity and customs. Most believe the Spanish language to be the single most important aspect of their heritage. And most Hispanics, whether they speak Spanish, English, or both, prefer to read in Spanish.

A 1983 audit conducted by Peat Marwick is included with the media kit, showing circulation as of December 31, 1983 to be at 116,177.

El Diario/La Prensa

Owned by the Gannett Company, *El Diario/La Prensa* is the largest Spanish-language newspaper in the United States. A daily newspaper providing the Hispanic community with in-depth analysis of the major local, national, and international news events, *El Diario/La Presna* is the result of a merger in 1963 of two competing New York dailies.

The oldest of the two, *La Prensa*, was established in 1913 by Jose Campubre, a Spaniard. It was bought by Fortune H. Pope in the latter part of the 50s. The other, *El Diario*, was established by Dr. Porfirio Dominicci in 1948 under the title *El Diario de Nueva York*.

In 1963, *El Diario* was acquired by O. Roy Chalk, who later that year purchased *La Prensa*. Several months later, he merged both newspapers to form *El Diario/La Prensa*.

In 1981, the Gannett Company purchased *El Diario/La Prensa* to gain access to the New York City market. Having established an eastern link, Gannett envisions *El Diario/La Prensa* as a nationwide Spanish-language news and information network, serving the country's fastest growing segment, the Hispanic market.

The backbone of the newspaper is its editorial page. Written in both Spanish and English, *El Diario* editorials analyze the issues that affect the Hispanic community. The paper's philosophy is one of responsible, objective, and informative journalism committed to voicing the Hispanic point of view.

El Diario's media kit also includes extensive research data compiled by Scarborough on the New York market, conducted in 1982. The report provides a demographic and lifestyle profile of the Hispanic print and broadcast media audiences. It also provides an in-depth analysis of their product usage levels and retail-store shopping patterns.

El Miami Herald

Headline, *New York Times*, May 11, 1987: "The Tough Question for The Herald Is in Spanish."

In 1976, *The Miami Herald* created an Hispanic supplement to respond to the needs of the Hispanic population in the Miami area: *El Miami Herald*. The publication offers translated versions of The Herald's editorials and is available only to those subscribers who request it. In mid-April 1987, *The Herald* launched a free Spanish-language publication featuring advertising, but no editorial content, called *El Anunciador*.

Whether *The Herald* will expand its Spanish-language coverage was up in the air as of summer 1987. A full study on the Hispanic market will soon be completed.

Noticias Del Mundo

Noticias del Mundo is America's only nationwide Spanish-language newspaper. Published via satellite, with separate daily editions serving New York, Los Angeles, San Francisco, Chicago, and other major cities, *Noticias* is a primary source of local, national, and international news and commentaries for the Hispanic-American.

Noticias' editorial coverage targets the information needs of educated, up-scale Hispanics who enjoy reading in their native language. It provides its readers with an information reservoir and focuses on the Hispanic community throughout the country.

Already established in two leading Hispanic markets, New York for five years, and Los Angeles for more than a year, *Noticias* began satellite publications in San Francisco and Chicago in 1986. It will establish future editions in Miami and San Antonio, providing a full national newspaper that penetrates all ethnic and geographic sections of the Hispanic marketplace.

According to its promotion, while the demographic patterns of each market area differ, the reader audience attracted to *Noticias del Mundo* is constant. Readers are Hispanics on the leading edge of the market's forward movement: more serious readers, better educated, with higher incomes, well integrated into American society but still interested in the cultural values of their native countries and their original language, Spanish.

In 1986, *Noticias* contracted with the Globe Research Corporation to conduct a reader survey. The results pointed to a highly loyal reader, who has been reading the paper for 3.8 years and chooses the paper 16-to-1 over the competition in the area. Forty-nine percent are in the 35-to-49-year-old bracket, representing prime purchasing power. Forty-seven percent report they have attended college or beyond, and the average family income is about 20 percent higher among readers of *Noticias* than the Hispanic average.

Also included in the kit is "Gateway to Hispanic Buying Power," a guidebook. It discusses the important ways advertisers can get the most for their advertising dollar through the print medium. The most striking point made: while readers are firm in their Hispanic heritage, their buying tastes and habits are a blend of Latin and modern American characteristics. Readers look to *Noticias* to serve all their information needs—news and features as well as consumer reports on products and services. Whether they are new arrivals or established community members, readers trust and rely on *Noticias del Mundo*.

In March 1987, *Noticias* introduced a "core-market circulation" program. The program's purpose is to target those Hispanic readers who account for the actual buying power and growth influence—those with disposable income.

In addition, *Noticias* provides an Hispanic-market newsletter to the advertising community called "ADVISTA." It is a monthly publication focusing on the Hispanic market, supplying advertising executives with information necessary to make the right choices in placement.

Although currently not audited, *Noticias* is in the process of choosing an auditing firm.

El Sol De Texas

One of Texas' weekly Hispanic newspapers (there are currently no daily Hispanic papers in the Texas area), *El Sol de Texas* has served the Dallas/Fort Worth area since 1966.

Although *El Sol De Texas* has not contracted for an independent market research report, statistics from outside sources, as well as comments from Texas community leaders and industry experts, give testament to a growing and lucrative Hispanic market in the Dallas/Fort Worth area. In that region:

- Over 75 percent of the Hispanics are under 35 years of age.

- 34 percent of the Spanish-speaking household heads have lived in the area for 20 years or more.
- More than 35 percent of the Hispanics are high-school graduates.
- 95 of the Hispanic households own at least one car; the average number of cars per household is two.
- More than two out of three Hispanic households in the market own their own homes.
- Two-thirds of all Hispanics in the area possess one or more credit cards.

The combined data indicate a recurring and overriding factor: the strength and endurance of the Spanish language. This, more than any other characteristic, is the unifying force linking Hispanics of all nationalities. Most of them think of themselves equally as Hispanics and Americans. They place great importance on perpetuating the Hispanic culture and language throughout succeeding generations, and are expressing a preference for Hispanic media.

HISPANIC TV/RADIO

Nightly on the Telemundo Spanish network's quiz show *La Piñata De Los $25,000*, contestants answer questions for the chance to swing at a cash-filled piñata that floats above the set.

Breaking the *piñata*, a tradition in Hispanic culture, may serve as a symbol for stateside Spanish-language media, for Hispanic television today is a battleground. Its potential rewards are so enormous that corporate raiders eye national networks and government agencies wage legal warfare to defend domestic ownership. Each contestant is attempting to break the *piñata* and reap the whirlwind of profits it holds.

Numbers count, and the numbers around Hispanic t.v. advertising, though poor at present, are rich in promise. In 1986, advertisers spent a mere $185,000,000 for spots on Spanish-language television—just a blip on the nation's t.v. screens, which draw more than $20 billion a year in English-language ad sales. But Reliance Group Holdings, Telemundo's parent company chaired by Saul P. Steinberg, estimates a *1,400 percent* increase by 1992, to $2.5 billion, as the Hispanic segment of the U.S. population approaches 10 percent.

Steinberg is not alone in his pursuit of Yanqui dollars from advertisers seeking Hispanic viewers. A joint venture of Hallmark Cards and First Chicago Venture Capital, seeking to purchase Hispanic television stations in ten cities, awaits approval from the Federal Communications Commission and resolution of shareholders' legal challenges. Other entrepreneurs have lines out for similar acquisitions.

SIN's Quarter Century

From 1962 to the recent past, Spanish-language television was dominated by a single entity, the Spanish International Network (SIN). Beginning with stations in San Antonio and Los Angeles, by 1986 SIN boasted more than 400 affiliates; many of them were low-powered UHF facilities or cable franchises, but an even dozen were high-profile and high-power channels in major Hispanic markets.

SIN's own research, conducted by the Miami-based Strategy Research Corporation (SRC), remains a popular source of information on Hispanic media habits. SIN has also led an ongoing argument over whether the methodology used by U.S. ratings systems properly measures the Hispanic television audience.

In the first regard, SIN's *Spanish USA* report gives a 1986 figure of 18.3 million Hispanics in the United States and a growth rate of 61 percent from 1970 to 1980—more than five times the national average. It is a younger market (50 percent more children, 25 percent more young adults than the general population) and one with larger families. Ninety percent of those age 16 or older are fluent in Spanish.

They watch television and listen to radio—half the time to Spanish-language broadcasts. An SRC study found an average of 2.4 hours daily viewing of Spanish-language television, 1.2 hours of listening to Hispanic radio stations. The numbers go up for the ages 18-to-34 audience segment: 2.7 hours of television, 1.4 hours of radio. And SIN claims to reach 82 percent of all Spanish households—a total of 4 million homes.

"The network is convinced that the diary and meter methodology used for Anglo television is—with the possible exception of two bilingual markets—ineffectual in the case of Spanish television," SIN charged in a separate report entitled *How to Measure the Viewing to Hispanic Television*. The time-honored diary systems employed by Nielsen and Arbitron were strongly challenged: "The nature of television has changed drastically, giving the viewer an appalling volume of additional viewing choices... Even the most conscientious diary-keeper must feel suffocated at the very prospect of trying to keep an accurate chronicle of viewing to these [new] myriads of channels."

SIN marshaled expert opinion. The strongest testimony came from former Arbitron general manager Norman Hecht: "It appears that the diary is dead, in a future that will see many more markets with multichannel cable systems." Added SIN: "If 'the diary is dead' in English t.v., it's even worse in Spanish t.v.! The problems faced by the diary methodolody in English-language television become absolutely overwhelming when one examines the unique requirements of the Spanish market."

The problems, according to SIN's report, are numerous. Contacts with Hispanic households are initiated in English; Spanish-language call-backs are "demeaning." Diary methods eliminate viewers with lesser education. Hispanics return diaries at approximately half the rate of the general market. Diary samples eliminate non-phone homes (a third of SIN's coverage-area population have no phones), so homes with phones are "overmeasured." Border markets such as El Paso-Juarez are miscounted.

SIN's report admits that meter measurement overcomes some of the flaws in the diary system, but by no means all. "There are not enough meters," says SIN. "SIN has no confidence in the small Spanish meter samples in the network's other [i.e., excepting Los Angeles and Miami] major bilingual markets: New York, San Francisco, Houston, etc." The border-area problems remain.

The SIN report goes on to boast of the methodologies of its own contracted research: time-tested, professional, reliable, and accurate. "In short, it works," reads the succinct final sentence of the report. Certainly it works to SIN's advantage, but that fact notwithstanding, SIN makes a good case—a case joined by other television and radio networks, English as well as Hispanic.

The count, of course, has enormous impact on rates. Many analysts of Hispanic market advertising expenditures insist that the investment of ad dollars is not keeping up with Hispanic buying power. A key indicator is the dollar amount spent by advertisers per 1,000 population: for the general population advertisers spend $100 per 1,000 population; for the Hispanic population, the figure is $1 per 1,000.

Certainly, Spanish-language television pulls the power spending among all dollars targeted for Hispanic advertising—46 percent of the total pie in 1986. But Hispanic broadcasters insist that the medium can support—indeed deserves—a much bigger buy.

"I don't want to sell time as a Spanish station," Carlos Barba, president and general manager of WNJU-TV, told *Advertising Today*. "I want to sell as a station that reaches 25 percent of the [New York] population."

Reaching that population, say Barba and his fellows, is a bargain of dimension. Those who sell time on Hispanic stations feel that miscounting the audience forces them to charge lower-than-fair rates. An A.C. Nielsen report comparing 1986 rates on early evening news shows listed a 30-second spot on English-language stations at $45,100; WXTV, telecasting from Paterson, New Jersey to New York's vast Hispanic audience, charged $1,000 for the same time.

Research activity has increased, says Peter Roslow, vice president and general manager of Information and Analysis, a research and ratings firm. Since 1985, research conducted by t.v. stations, advertisers, and research services has doubled. According to a former vice president and director of sales for SIN, John Pero, "It's just a big fallacy that there's not enough research out there to support the Hispanic buy . . . It's a growing market, and it continues to grow."

Style and Substance

But if SIN complained about the measurement of its viewers, there were SIN viewers with important complaints about the quality of SIN's programming—complaints that have played a part in unfriendly takeover bids.

Through 1986 the greater part of SIN's programming came from Mexico's largest broadcaster, Televisa, which owned 75 percent of SIN. Soap operas, films, and entertainment with a distinct Las Vegas touch dominated, intercut with live and taped sporting events. News programming supplied by Televisa naturally focused on Mexican affairs—of little interest to Hispanics on the East Coast with ties to Puerto Rico, Cuba, and Central and South America. *Noticiero SIN*, the network's own evening news, charted a different and more far-ranging course, but its independence was threatened in 1986 when SIN announced that *Noticiero SIN* would be placed under an international news agency based in Mexico.

In any case, news—however well produced—claimed but a small part of SIN's daily fare. Far more common were escapist programs with little revelance to Hispanic life in the United States. A Los Angeles-based Hispanic-American group made that complaint central to their attempt to buy a number of key SIN affiliates. "There should be a variety of programs directed towards the Hispanic community itself," Dr. Tirso del Junco, the group's leader, told *Hispanic Business* in late 1986. "You could have more educational programs, more shows of interest to the community."

Mexican ownership had ramifications beyond the quality and subject of programming. SIN's affiliates in New York, Los Angeles, Miami, San Francisco, and five smaller localities were owned by a single company, the Spanish International Communication Corporation (SICC). SICC and SIN shared offices and phones in New York. This interlock, along with questions of stock ownership and the presence of individuals involved in both station and network management, drew the eye of the Federal Communications Commission. FCC rules limit foreign ownership of U.S. stations (but not networks that supply the stations with programs) to 20 percent.

Consequently, the FCC denied renewal of licenses to 11 SIN affiliates and ordered SICC to divest itself of 7 affiliate stations. The Hallmark-First Chicago partnership was eager to buy 10 affiliates in six cities. Although the sales are under challenge from Hispanic groups objecting to the new ownership—they believe minority ownership of minority-focused stations is in order—the Hallmark deal seems certain of approval. *Hispanic Business* writer Steve Beale told AMA in July 1987: "Just about all obstacles have been removed. The denial of licenses to SIN affiliates has been an obstacle to the sale, and would mandate that they be sold at a 'distress price.' But the licenses have been approved."

Attorney Bruce Eisen, representing the Coalition for Preserving Hispanic Broadcasting, is less certain of the final resolution. "It's still pending," Eisen points out; his clients have filed a notice of appeal.

The probable outcome: SICC will sell the stations to Hallmark, and SIN will continue to provide programming and to sell commercial time on its network. The judge hearing the case has said that past infractions were not serious and could be resolved by restructuring the relationship between SICC and SIN.

SIN No More

Amid suits and countersuits and preliminary injunctions, and with new competition on the horizon from the Steinberg group, it seemed the better part of valor for SIN to reorganize in a major way. First priority: a change in name.

The network name itself had long been a problem. As *Hispanic Business* explained it, "In English... a *sin* is a breach of conduct, while in Spanish, it means *without*." "SIN" was dropped, and in November 1986 the new name—Univision—was announced in *Television/Radio Age*. "Introducing a spanking new t.v. network with a 25-year-old history," read the front cover of the magazine's close-up on the Hispanic market. There was a new blue-and-white logo featured as well as a new slogan: "One vision, one language, one network: Univision. The network that Spanish U.S.A. calls its own."

Its own perhaps, but no longer its only. In January 1987, the Reliance holdings joined the fray under the corporate flag of Telemundo Group, Inc. Telemundo is the child of station buyouts in New York, Los Angeles, Miami, and Puerto Rico. By its own figuring, Telemundo begins with a reach covering one-third of the domestic Hispanic population, and it aims for additional links to make penetration total.

Important to the Telemundo challenge is original programming out of New York and Los Angeles, as well as purchased material and live sporting events from Puerto Rico, Mexico, Argentina, and Venezuela. SIN-style programming, heavy on soap operas and entertainment, has been the mode for decades. And in most markets it was SIN programming or none at all—few independent challengers existed.

In the last few years, independents such as KVEA Channel 52 in Los Angeles and WSCU Channel 51 in Miami have joined the foremost non-SIN outlet, New York's WNJU, to take a considerable share of audience and ad revenues from SIN's network. Says *Hispanic Business*: "Independent television has dramatically increased its share of advertising dollars from $20.5 million to $42.3 million in the last year." KVEA claims 35 percent of Los Angeles Hispanic viewers, and WSCU reports a 40 percent share of Miami Hispanics.

All of these independents have been bought by the Reliance Group for Telemundo. Part of that deal included Net-Span, WNJU's programming and sales rep service. Using Net-Span services, Telemundo will offer flexible programming to local affiliates, segmenting its offerings by local ethnic origin. A *novela*—English-language audiences would call them soap operas—for a Los Angeles audience may feature a Mexican slant, which would differ from Telemundo's *novelas* in Miami, where a Cuban background would be more apt. That, in turn, would differ from what New York's largely Puerto Rican audience would view. SIN's audience, of course, has not received such differentiated programming.

The next decade will see a face-off between Telemundo and the stations owned by Hallmark which take their programs from Univision, heir to SIN. In the three leading Hispanic markets, Univision and Telemundo programming will go head to head.

The Big Three

Los Angeles has 873,000 Hispanic households that own televisions. It remains the foremost Hispanic market in the domestic U.S.A. Upstart KVEA, which began broadcasting in 1985, claims a 35 percent share of the Angeleno Hispanic t.v. audience and anticipated $9.5 million in ad dollars in 1986. The Reliance Group bought the station in 1986 for $38 million.

Like the other independents, KVEA emphasizes local programming. Among its exclusives was live coverage of the annual East Los Angeles Parade, a central event in the heart of LA's Hispanic community. Pursuing a strategy of counterprogramming against SIN's offerings—that is, playing off the schedule of its competitor by running programs of opposite type—KVEA aims for command of the LA market by 1990.

Univision affiliate KMEX, Channel 34 in Los Angeles, boasted ad sales of $36 million in 1986, a 30 percent jump from the previous year. Among KMEX's triumphs was coverage of the World Cup final soccer match between Mexico and West Germany, which drew an audience of 282,000 households —beating all the major English-language stations in the same time slot.

New York, the second largest Hispanic market, with three-quarters of a million households having televisions, continues the rivalry between Univision affiliate WNJU and Telemundo's WXTV. The former receives higher audience ratings, but not all its viewers are Hispanic; WNJU sells time to other second-language broadcasters. Because of that, its ad revenues trail WXTV's. The Telemundo outlet sold $20 million worth of time in 1986, compared to $13.5 million for WNJU. Arbitron gives both stations an equal share of the Hispanic audience; Strategy Research grants WNJU a slight edge.

Miami runs third to LA and New York, but it is seen as the "softest" market in the big three, due to the slowdown in Hispanic immigration and the troubled economy in once-booming southern Florida. The Hispanic audience: 281,000 households with televisions.

In spite of the economic downturn, neither of the two Hispanic television stations is complaining. WSCV Channel 51, a subsidiary of the John Blair Company before its sale to Reliance and consequent link with Telemundo, has gained a 40 percent share of the Hispanic audience since it went on the air in 1985. WLTV, a Univision affiliate up for sale to Hallmark, is the traditional leader; it grabbed $23.6 million in ad sales in 1986.

More markets will entertain the Univision-Telemundo rivalry in future years. Low-power stations and cable outlets will enter the lists as well. Within a decade, the field that SIN once held for itself will witness fierce rivalry and eventual shakeout—will come to resemble, in fact, the state of Hispanic radio broadcasting.

HISPANIC RADIO

What can radio do that t.v. can't? Many advertisers in the Hispanic market hold that radio offers decided advantages over the other media. Giving radio the edge are such factors as flexibility, reach, round-the-clock access, and economy—a better cost per thousand.

Whereas most television programming has originated outside U.S. borders, Spanish-language radio originates in the home market and can thereby gear its format to a particular audience. Hispanics in California—predominantly "Chicanos" from Mexico, with a recent influx from Central America—differ culturally, and thus in their program choices, from the Puerto Rican communities of New York and the Cuban populations of southern Florida. While the language itself is a common denominator, national variations and distinction in accent do make for differences, and advertisers ignore such differences at their peril.

The demarkations are easy to identify. Ninety percent of all Hispanics live in ten states; of those, 71 percent live in four major markets (New York, California, Florida, and Texas).

According to *U.S. Hispanic Affairs*, "experts generally agree that radio reaches approximately 85 percent of the U.S. Hispanic population." And a 1986 Arbitron report, entitled *Radio Today: The Hispanic Listener*, concluded that radio reached 98 percent of Hispanics age 12 and above every week. According to the Arbitron report, the average listener devotes 30 hours per week to the radio.

Long-time players are convinced that radio advertising works. Anheuser-Busch, Sears, and McDonald's have skillfully tapped radio's potential. Bristol-Myers tested the waters in the spring of 1985 and came away convinced. The pharmaceutical giant sought to measure how sales of Ban Roll-On and Excedrin were affected by Spanish-language radio advertising on selected local radio stations. The test compared sales in markets receiving the Spanish ads against those that did not. The results:

- For Ban Roll-On, the Spanish-language campaign increased market share by 3 percent—an increase larger than Ban's growth in the general market. Markets outside the test zone showed no gain.

- For Excedrin, the expected winter share decline was less in areas receiving the Spanish-language ads than for those outside the test zone, as well as being less than the decline the product suffered in the general market.

According to Bristol-Myers vice president Peter Spengler, speaking to *Hispanic Business:* "We're encouraged by the continued growth in size and purchasing power in the Hispanic population. Hispanic media is now an established support effort for many of our brands. As successful marketers, we can do no less than to continue our efforts in the Hispanic market, thereby enlarging our own experience and success as the marketing man's dream blossoms into full reality in coming years."

Other advertisers are convinced that the economics of Spanish radio advertising provide distinct advantages. "More Firms Tune in to Radio to Stretch Their Ad Budgets," the *Wall Street Journal* headlined in July 1986, reporting that rates for Spanish-language radio offer a considerably lower CPM than mainstream radio.

Arbitron studied radio audiences by day parts and found that young people represent the majority of overnight listeners, whereas older audiences predominate during the day and evening. Spanish radio, observers agree, draws a generally older audience. Spanish broadcast schedules are built around music programs; Hispanic teens, as they assimiliate into the mainstream, tend to listen to Anglo stations for the latest hits. Older Hispanics, on the other hand, remain loyal to their musical heritage, be it salsa, mariachi, or Tex-Mex country.

The argument over accurate audience counts appears less bitter where radio ratings are concerned than when Hispanic television viewers are involved. This is a result of direct action by Hispanic radio reps. Led by Eduardo Cabellero, whose Cabellero Spanish Media organization both sells time and packages programs for a national consortium of Spanish-language radio stations, an impressive roster of Hispanic business leaders formed the Spanish Radio Advisory Council in 1986. The goal: to "do something about the 'Arbitron Issue' "—the thesis that Arbitron's diary method and dependence on telephone listings severly undercount Spanish listeners.

The council chose the Hicksville, New York firm of Information and Analysis, Inc. to conduct listener surveys in most major Hispanic markets. Their research continues as they test various methodologies; door-to-door interviews by Hispanic researchers, although expensive, seem to hold the best promise for an accurate count.

This is not the first time Hispanic broadcasters have joined together to challenge the establishment. In 1980, the Spanish Radio Broadcasters of America (SRBA) petitioned the Federal Communications Commission to withdraw a waiver it had granted to the Spanish International Communications Corporation (SICC), main programming supplier to the SIN television network. The effect of the waiver was that it gave SICC an enormous advantage in negotiating ad sales, ultimately leaving radio stations at a severe disadvantage.

FCC action on the petition was postponed pending settlement of the foreign control petition brought against SICC (see reportage in the television section above). Meanwhile, SICC countered with an antitrust suit against the SRBA, charging that the intent of their 1980 petition was to inhibit competiton. Final settlement awarded legal expenses to the SRBA, but nothing more—a bitter disappointment to the radio broadcasters which severely diminished the SRBA's effectiveness. Vindication may be in sight: SICC's waiver is scheduled to be removed pending the FCC's final approval of the Hallmark sale reported above.

Eduardo Cabellero looks forward to that day. "There is no way I can express what this will mean for advertising revenues for other Spanish-language media once it [the waiver] is done away with," Cabellero says.

Cabellero's stake is major. His companies sell advertising for more than 60 independently owned and operated Spanish-language radio stations across the nation. It offers advertisers access to the entire network or to any combination of stations. In some cases it is the exclusive national representative for a station; in others it shares representation. CSM identifies its client list as the *Caballero Radio Network*, although in the classic sense the group is not a broadcast network. CSM also packages short program spots which are pre-sold to advertisers and then distributed to its client stations.

Eduardo Caballero, with an 11-year background in advertising sales for Spanish-language radio and television, began CSM in 1973 as a syndicator of Spanish-language t.v. shows. At the request of various t.v. stations, he began representing them to advertisers, adding radio stations to his list. By 1976, with radio showing a larger growth potential ("Nobody was *selling* radio time to national clients"), Caballero dropped his t.v. station clients to concentrate exclusively on radio—the first, he says, to do so.

Finding that advertising agencies were not interested in buying spots on one or two or even as many as a half-dozen Spanish-language stations, Caballero set out to gather the largest possible client list. This required shared representation with other reps, with Caballero selling time on a "network" basis—that is, offering advertisers a *combination* of stations—while *individual* stations continued with their prior representation. This remains Caballero's practice.

"Numbers vary according to the souce," Cabellero comments on the ratings game. "We know where Hispanic populations are concentrated, but little else beyond that. The constant influx of Hispanics into the United States makes it difficult to know more. The market changes so rapidly that research is often obsolete by the time it's published.

"Moreover, researchers are dealing with a culture that does not react in a conventional way to researchers or research methodologies. As a member of Arbitron's bilingual review board, I know this to be true. I am often embarrassed when I am asked standard questions about demographics and spending patterns, because we are unable to answer with any exactitude.

"This has been a long-standing problem with the rating services," Cabellero continues. "Our advisory council, and our association with Information Analysis, we hope will yield correct figures. The first results from a pilot project in Chicago that used different methodologies are due very soon, and with this kind of sponsorship we should have no problems of credibility.

"But there are questions beyond ratings," Cabellero warns. "How can we determine if a product is being used? What effect does a Spanish-language campaign have in a mixed market? Are advertisers buying efficiently and effectively? How can a client do a competitive analysis? Ultimately these questions will be answered. More resources will be put into this research as the potential of the market becomes more obvious.

"That is happening. If I had attempted to form such a council two or three years ago, perhaps my phone calls would not have been returned. And when one sees a company like Procter and Gamble, which is usually very conservative and cautious, getting into the Hispanic market—not simply with advertising, but creating a fully staffed in-house Hispanic marketing department, you realize that other companies will not be far behind."

Although the scope of Cabellero's enterprise is nationwide, the Hispanic market remains tightly packed into four key markets. A brief review of the players in those areas is in order here.

Miami: Although third in size of the big three Hispanic markets, Miami is home of the top revenue earner in radio, WQBA-FM, and boasts the most crowded radio market, with eight stations. WQBA's reported revenues in 1986 were between $10 million and $11 million. The city has become the capital of the Hispanic music recording industry, which in part accounts for the large number of stations.

Most of the station's revenues come from 1,500 local advertisers. Says Guillermo Mota, WQBA's general manager, "We have more advertising revenues from local retailers than any other station in the United States—general-market or Spanish-language." Once national advertisers learn to tap this potential, Moto predicts, ad rates will become equivalent with those of Anglo stations.

Los Angeles: Close on the heels of WQBA in Miami in terms of revenues is LA's KLVE-FM, which forms an AM-FM combo with KTNQ. KLVE has the distinction of being the only Hispanic station to counter the 1986 trend of lower growth in revenues over previous years. Since its purchase by H&W Communications in 1985, the FM station has doubled its listenership, catapulting it into the big league. It ranks tenth in popularity in the general LA radio market. According to the *Los Angeles Herald*, "It is believed to be the first time a Spanish station cracked the top ten."

As LA's other stations grow more competitive, KLVE has instituted programming changes that account for its rapid growth. Sports coverage has been cut in favor of music, generally agreed to be the staple of Spanish radio. With the H&W takeover, KTNQ was positioned as the information outlet of the combo. The music format is now international, drawing Mexican, South American, and Central American audiences, with a U.S. "top 40" format to reach teenagers and families. Commercial time was cut drastically to 12 minutes an hour. Signal improvements now allow the station to reach a larger area.

Chicago: For years the Hispanic market in Chicago had been a well-kept secret. Predominantly Mexican with some Puerto Ricans and Cubans, the 1.1 million Chicago Hispanics have been largely ignored. However, a recent wave of new media outlets has focused new attention on the city.

Two new radio stations, WTAQ-FM and WIND-AM, will now test their mettle against WOJO-FM, long the only player in the market.

Broadcasting in Spanish since 1968, WOJO uses "international" Spanish because of the ethnic mix of its audience. The two new stations were quick to take hold, introducing lively competition for WOJO. The competition has already fanned the fires, and the market has gained in national advertisers. Previously, only Budweiser, Miller, and Coca-Cola advertised on WOJO. Now other nationals including Coors, Ford, Libby, and some cigarette brands have emerged on the other outlets.

New York: The second-largest Hispanic market, New York is home to a rapidly changing Hispanic population. Most estimates add a half-million to one million to the Census figure of 2 million Hispanic New Yorkers to help account for the undocumented numbers. At one time Puerto Ricans made up 80 percent of this immigrant group and their descendants; they now comprise 46.5 percent, according to a Media Institute study, *Hispanic Media, U.S.A.,* by Ana Veciana Suarez. "Dominicans rank second with 26.7 percent, Central and South Americans 2.2 percent, Cubans 7.2 percent, Mexicans 2.2 percent, and Spaniards less than one percent." Strategy Research data place 36 percent under age 18 and 70 percent under 35—young, but not as young as LA Hispanics.

In the race to dominate the New York airwaves, WADO continues to maintain a substantial lead over the other three full-time Spanish-language radio stations in the market—WKDM, WSKQ, and WJIT. WKDM and WSKQ are neck in neck for second place, with WJIT trailing as third.

In 1986, WADO was the object of a would-be record-breaking sale to Tichenor Media System for $20 million. A last-minute snafu prevented the sale from going through. However, it almost made broadcasting history. The media, reporting it as a *fait accompli*, touted the purchase price as the highest for a standalone AM station in the history of broadcasting.

WADO presents a blend of musical styles, emphasizing international hits of Latin America, as opposed to the Hispanic staple, salsa. News and talk focus on Latin American and U.S. Latinos.

The typical WADO listener is female, over 25 years old. In an average quarter-hour, according to Arbitron's winter 1986 ratings, the station attracts 48,300 listeners. The majority (60 percent) of the station's advertisers are national companies.

The station is, as of this writing, negotiating another sale.

WKDM dubs itself "Radio Musical." Its average quarter-hour listenership, 29,800, ranks it in second place with WSKQ close behind. In 1986 the station, then WBNX, had its call letters changed, and at the same time upgraded its programming to make it more competitive.

According to its media kit, "Now, for the first time in the New York market a Latin radio station is programmed with general-market competitive techniques. WKDM presents an uptempo, wall of sound, flow-oriented music presentation." News and information are broadcast approximately every 30 minutes during the daytime hours.

Like WADO's audience, WKDM's listeners are primarily women (ages 18 to 34), but the station also draws a substantial male audience (ages 18 to 34). Advertising is heavily national, but local ads also claim a strong portion.

5

Met Life: Across the Board

"METROPOLITAN STANDS BY YOU"

The old standby slogan of Metropolitan Life Insurance is making a comeback—in the ethnic marketplace.

Met Life is currently achieving pronounced inroads into the Hispanic- and Asian-language markets throughout the United States. According to Ruben Lopez, market director of personal insurance sales for Metropolitan Life, "Right now it is extremely competitive out there, especially in the insurance and financial services market. Brokerage houses, insurance companies, and banking institutions are all getting into each other's areas of expertise. In order to differentiate ourselves from the pack, we've turned to ethnic target marketing—to appeal to these lucrative groups in their own language."

The concept has proved successful for Met in the past. During the late 1800s, a period of increased European immigration, sales agents prepared promotion literature in such languages as Italian and German to attract these new arrivals. When immigration tapered off, the idea was dropped. Now it is being revived with the target focusing on Hispanics and Asians.

A NATION WITHIN A NATION

This new round of target marketing began in 1983, with a proposal by the former marketing director of special projects, Jose Gastal-Garcia. At the time, he was with the international division and was assigned to look at foreign markets abroad, with an eye toward establishing niches in overseas markets for Metropolitan's products and services. What he discovered was a substantial untapped market in the domestic United States—a nation within a nation—the Hispanic-American market.

Gastal-Garcia was given the opportunity to run free with the idea and develop a marketing strategy aimed at this group. In April 1983, Strategy Research Corporation of Miami conducted comprehensive research consisting of focus groups and person-to-person interviews in the major Hispanic centers around the country. The research raised questions regarding purchasing patterns and reasons individuals choose one company's services over another. The results indicated that the Hispanic population was young, family-oriented, and up and coming and would be the ideal market for Met's insurance products.

These interviews supplied information not only on the financial aspect of the group but on marketing strategy as well. The findings provided Met Life with numbers to back the assumptions that Hispanics prefer to be marketed to in their native language. In fact, addressing Hispanic consumers in Spanish was particularly important for a company like Metropolitan. Attracting these people away from competitors was not enough; they also had to sell them on the benefits of insurance and financial services, concepts that are difficult enough to understand, without the added barrier of language.

THE HISPANIC MARKET

Although the Hispanic community presented itself as an ideal market for Metropolitan's services, successful marketing would require careful planning. The consequences of jumping in and making mistakes could be disastrous, either alienating the community from the company or, in other instances, the company from the community. Met Life chose to enter slowly by test marketing in two major Hispanic centers: Miami and San Antonio. With a small nucleus of 20 Hispanic sales representatives, Met set out to convert the Hispanic way of thinking—to make the idea of insurance and investment more familiar and comfortable to Hispanic consumers.

And the effort proved successful. Hispanic sales representatives were able to inform their potential clients about their services in a language they could understand, as well as provide translated sales and promotion literature. The results were very encouraging, according to Lopez, with the Hispanic reps getting better results in their areas than their non-Hispanic counterparts.

Because of its success, Met decided to roll out the project into additional Hispanic communities, and in 1984 it targeted the Los Angeles market. According to Lopez, this marked Metropolitan Life's commitment to the Hispanic market. With more than 3 million Hispanic residents, the Los Angeles metropolitan area is the largest Hispanic center in the United States. In addressing these numbers, the success or failure of the entire project would be determined.

With this expansion, Metropolitan increased its Hispanic sales representation from 20 to 45, and in 1985, when the campaign went national, representation rose to 94. Currently, Met employs 225 Hispanic sales reps to service these consumers, with the heaviest concentration in the seven largest Hispanic centers (Los Angeles, Miami, San Antonio, Houston, San Francisco, New York, and Chicago).

Successful Marketing to U.S. Hispanics & Asians

Metropolitan.
El primer paso hacia un futuro mejor.

Usted puede escalar hasta la cima del éxito profesional como Representante de Ventas de Metropolitan. Donde usted podrá mejorar su posición y multiplicar sus ingresos sin límite.

Tenemos uno de los mejores programas de entrenamiento en la materia y el respaldo de más de 100 años de experiencia.

Administramos más de 94 mil millones de dólares en activos y más de 44 millones de personas están aseguradas con Metropolitan y sus afiliadas.

¡Dé el primer paso ahora!...¡llámenos!

1-800-638-6060

IGUALDAD EN OPORTUNIDAD DE EMPLEO

Metropolitan Life AND AFFILIATED COMPANIES

Metropolitan. The first step toward a better future.

MAKE THE FIRST STEP NOW! CALL US!

Metropolitan Life's recruitment advertisement, for the Hispanic market, created by the Conill Advertising Agency, New York.

Met Life: Across the Board

By the end of 1985, Met Life's success in the market was fully realized. Research showed that market awareness of Metropolitan Life among Hispanics had jumped from a distant fourth among insurace companies to first.

In 1985, Ruben Lopez joined the program as project director. He explains, "As the campaign went into full force, Metropolitan felt that it needed someone with field experience to bring a new perspective to the project. At that point I had been with the company for about ten years, moving up from a sales representative, to sales manager, and eventually to branch manager."

According to Lopez, reaching the Hispanic market has been a complete success story. "The numbers keep increasing, not only in market share, but in sales representatives and premium dollars as well. In a 1986 follow-up market survey, results indicated that we had maintained our market share position from 1985, and that market awareness among the group had increased by 7 percent (from 35 to 42 percent)."

Lopez adds, "In addition, 1986 premiums were up by 15 percent from the previous year. This in itself is amazing. The insurance industry as a whole increased by 5 percent at the most last year—with Met Life in general increasing by 11 percent. The 15 percent in the Hispanic market is phenomenal compared to the other statistics in the industry."

Strategy Research Corporation, based in Miami, conducted most of Metropolitan Life's Hispanic market research. These studies are repeated on a yearly basis, using a database of 1,400 Hispanic households (200 from each of the seven Hispanic target markets). The interviews are conducted in the field, with face-to-face questioning, and provide constant feedback on the community's attitude toward the company, in addition to informaton on its evolution.

The Advertising Picture

Initially, Metropolitan Life addressed its Hispanic consumers through its sales representatives. But, to attract any significant group—and obviously this includes Hispanics, with a population of more than 20 million—mass-media advertising is certainly the route to go. According to Lopez, current promotion involves all areas of the media: television, radio, and print. Of these, television is Met's most significant media channel.

To head up its Hispanic marketing, Met chose two New York agencies—Conill, and Grau and Garcia. Their combined advertising savvy created the "genie" spokesperson for Metropolitan—the Hispanic counterpart to the Anglo *Snoopy* campaign. Occasionally, Metropolitan uses Snoopy in its Hispanic campaigns, but it's the genie that provides the recognition for Met in the Hispanic market. A recent survey revealed a 55 percent awareness rate among Hispanics in connecting the genie with Metropolitan Life.

The genie campaign was a stroke of genius on the agencies' part. According to Lopez, "This was a case where translation peculiarities worked in the company's favor. The word "genie" in Spanish is *genio*, which also translates to mean "genius." The ad translates: 'You don't have to be a genie/genius to know that the future of your family is your primary concern.' It became a double bonus.

"I believe that sensitivity is the key to any advertising effort. With the Hispanic market we can be cute and humorous, as we are with the Anglo market. But we also need to inform and present information in a format that Hispanics can understand."

The genie campaign was designed to educate the Hispanic consumer on the importance of insurance. The message is that the genie is all-knowing and all-powerful. At times they use humorous situations—where the genie is in dangerous situations, but because of his powers he gets out unharmed. The idea is if you're not a genie then you need insurance. The campaign was developed back in 1983, and since then the genie has grown, with a wife and a family. Currently, only Grau and Garcia are handling the campaign.

Metropolitan sent out its genie campaign full force into the Hispanic media, appearing on Hispanic television and radio, as well as in popular Hispanic print channels, including local newspapers and monthly magazines, among them *Hispanic Business, Hispanic Review of Business*, and *Selecciones* (the Hispanic edition of *Readers Digest*). Although most of the ads appear in Spanish, Met does run ads created in English that have an Hispanic flavor. One ad, which features Snoopy and Lucy, has Snoopy saying, "Hola, sweetie, guess who's No. 1 in the top Hispanic markets." According to Lopez, "By using English in Hispanic ads, we are addressing the Hispanic-American as a whole person. Many of the Hispanics living in the United States want that feeling of assimilation that comes from speaking one language, yet they still want to maintain their Hispanic heritage. This allows us to recognize them as Hispanic-Americans."

In 1986, the campaign moved away from promoting the concept of insurance to a smaller platform of promoting specific products. Items such as term, whole life, and Universal life insurance policies are the big sellers in the Hispanic market, and as such are the ones highlighted in their product seller advertisements, featured in *Seleccionnes*. This is working very well for Met. According to Lopez, ads they ran as far back as August 1986 are still getting replies. In 1987, Met plans to start using the genie in promoting specific products, with Universal life being the kick-off product.

In addition to product advertisement, Met has also begun recruitment advertising in the Hispanic market. One ad stating "First step to a better future," depicts feet walking up building blocks that carry the Met logo. Another ad features five men on a race track, with one in a suit: "If your goal is success, you're on the right track with Met." In addition to running the ads in Spanish in the regular Hispanic media, Met features the ads in English as well, in such publications as *Vista* and *Hispanic Business*—appealing to the English-dominant Hispanic.

Is this Market Lucrative?

It's a question that is being asked by many marketing directors throughout the United States, and Lopez's answer is yes. "I was quoted in *Advertising Age* as saying, and I'll stand behind it, that once Hispanics have been in this country ten years or more, their income tends to equal and in many instances exceed that of their non-Hispanic counterparts."

Current statistics show that the Hispanic population is growing tremendously from one year to the next. Combined with the assumption that there are many undocumented Hispanics in this country, the population figure of 20 million is underestimated. Current income figures for Hispanics are much lower than the national average, but the group tends to spend more of its disposable income than the average.

Community Involvement: U.S. Hispanic Chamber of Commerce

The recent endorsement Metropolitan Life received from the U.S. Hispanic Chamber of Commerce, a membership organization of 500,000 Hispanic-owned businesses, is proof of its success in the Hispanic market. Its endorsement by the chamber, based in Kansas City, Missouri, gives Met sole rights to the chamber's mailing list for use in soliciting new clients.

Metropolitan is also involved in other Hispanic community events, such as Jobs for Progress, La Raza, and the U.S. Hispanic Chamber of Commerce Convention. All these groups have benefited from participation or sponsorship from Met. These involvements are positive for Metropolitan as well, providing an additional outlet for the company to promote its services, and increase its name recognition in the community.

Once Met had successfully penetrated the Hispanic market, it went on to look for new and exciting markets that would both stretch its marketing boundaries and provide increased revenues.

THE ASIAN MARKET

In 1985, after successfully penetrating the Hispanic market, Metropolitan decided to branch out into other areas of ethnic marketing. The Asian market was the most logical step. Much of what had been done in the Hispanic market now needed to be fit into the Asian mindset.

But why target the Asians? Metropolitan saw it this way. As a minority group, their numbers equal 5.5 million, with projections for the next few years targeting a phenonmenal growth rate (14 times faster than that of the general population). In the next 20 years the numbers will double, according to some estimates.

It's not only sheer numbers that make this group appealing. Asians have high potential purchasing power and a high rate of assimilation. On the whole their median family income is significantly greater than that of other minorities, at $22,075 per year—compared to $19,908 for the general population. In addition, 31.6 percent of all Asians have four or more years of college, versus 16.3 percent of the general population. One-fifth of all minorities who own their own businesses are Asian. In general these numbers point to a significant consumer market, one that will be interested in more up-scale products.

Unlike Met Life's efforts in the Hispanic market, which began from scratch, the Asian market project had a step up on the ladder. When they began in 1985, Met already had 300 Asian sales representatives in place, successfully penetrating the market with their operations.

Another factor that influenced Met's decision to target this market had to do with its success without marketing. In 1984, the top Metropolitan Life sales office in premium revenue was their Far West branch in Los Angeles, run by Ray Ting, who is Chinese. And in 1985, it was a sales office in Houston, run by Tai Chang, who is Korean.

These representatives proved to be a vital element in Metropolitan's understanding of the Asian market. Settled and already addressing the consumer, they were able to provide the company with important marketing knowledge that had proved difficult to compile for the Asian community.

Successful Marketing to U.S. Hispanics & Asians

Welcome to Met Life's Nationwide Family of 44 Million.

44 MILLION SATISFIED CUSTOMERS ARE YOUR BEST REASON TO GET MET.

Ad campaign designed to improve Metropolitan's image in the Asian communities. This version, in Korean, was created by L3 Advertising, New York.

Met Life: Across the Board

A portion of the marketing research on Asians was conducted by Langer Associates, a market research company based in New York City. According to Alan Levin, a researcher with Langer, gaining information about Asians is difficult in the best conditions. "Telephone interviews, mail surveys, and in-person interviews are the primary ways information is gained. Most Asians are reluctant to give information, and this is especially true when they are dealing with non-Asian personnel—and using a translator is less than ideal."

For their information, Langer Associates interviewed Metropolitan Life's Asian sales representatives. They wanted to make use of their personal knowledge of the culture and gain information about the customers, the kinds of insurance they were most interested in, and the types of protection they were looking for. According to Levin, although this was not the ideal way to gain information, it did yield fairly accurate results that held up.

The groups studied were the Chinese, Vietnamese, Korean, and Filipino. The study provided three focal points of information that would be helpful in creating a successful marketing plan in the Asian market. The factors that surfaced were:

- A strong desire to set up an education fund for children,
- A reluctance to accept insurance and financial institutions, and
- The importance of working with a company that is No. 1.

According to Levin, the question that came up most frequently was a concept the Asian respondents termed "education insurance." Here the Asian consumer was inquiring about a policy that would guarantee payment for their children's and grandchildren's college education. The concept of achievement proved to be a high priority among many Asian immigrants.

The second point, their reluctance to accept financial institutions, stems from homeland experience. Many Asian immigrants are from countries where only the very wealthy can afford these services, or from countries where a lack of government regulation in these operations has created mismanagement or corruption, resulting in fraud or collapse. One of Metropolitan's priorities was to re-educate Asian consumers in the concept of insurance and make them feel comfortable about investing and secure in the protection of their assets. The concept of security of principle rates highly when Asian consumers consider investments.

The third point is the concept of being No. 1. According to the Langer study, a company that promotes itself as being No. 1—the biggest, having the most assets, managing the most investments—is the company that is going to gain these investors.

But it's not only that the company needs to be perceived as being successful. Representatives also need a record of success in their own departments. According to one of the Korean sales representatives, when dealing with an Asian client, "It is important to stress some area where either the agent or the entire sales office is No. 1 within a larger group. For example, that the agent is No. 1 in his office, or that the office (with Asian personnel) is No. 1 in the country."

In this area Metropolitan has been successful. Sales offices staffed and operated by Asian personnel were No. 1 in the country in 1984, 1985 and 1986.

The 1985 Campaign

When Met made its initial move into the Asian marketplace, it directed the marketing to two subsets of the Asian community: Chinese and Korean. The base of their marketing to these groups was print (primarily newspaper) and community involvement. Met targeted nine Asian communities: Los Angeles, San Francisco, Seattle, Washington, Houston, Philadelphia, New York, Chicago, Washington, D.C., and Boston.

Advertising for the market is currently handled by L3, a full-service Asian advertising agency based in New York's Chinatown. The original thrust of the campaign was to create a corporate recognition for Metropolitan Life in the Asian communities throughout the United States. According to Joseph Lam, a partner at L3, "As big as Metropolitan has been in the United States, it is relatively obscure in the Asian communities. Other, smaller insurance companies were more well known, because they had installed Asian agents in the communities and were more aggressive in terms of personal selling. When we got the account, we felt that the first step in the campaign was to build up the image of Met in the community. It became the first step in an overall three-step process."

Image Builder

The first step, termed an "image builder," was designed to capitalize on Met's existing position in the financial community. The headline reads: "Welcome to Met Life's Nationwide Family of 44 Million," and proceeds to inform the reader about the depth of Met's financial management. Stability and strength are the concepts highlighted in this initial campaign, in order to make the consumer more comfortable with investing.

The Educator

Once consumers were made aware of the company and its stability, the campaign followed with education on the benefits of buying insurance. According to Lam, this presented a catch-22 situation for Metropolitan. "For the most part, you sell insurance on the basis of death—a protection device for your family when you are no longer there—but Asians are very superstitious, with death being a subject they are reluctant to discuss. To get around this, we chose to use their children, with the emphasis on protection. The ad read: 'You protect your baby. Who protects you?'" In addressing the Asian consumer on the basis of their commitment to their family, Metropolitan is recognizing the family-oriented nature of the immigrant group.

Product Seller

The third step in the L3 plan was termed a "product seller." In this instance, the ads highlighted a particular insurance product that L3 felt would be well received in the community. One product that research showed to have popularity among Asians was Universal life insurance. To capitalize on its existing popularity, Metropolitan ran ads promoting the product with the tagline: "Interest yourself in more than interest."

The three-step process was designed to bring the community to a complete understanding of the products and services that Metropolitan offers. Advertising in this way seemed very important within

Met Life: Across the Board

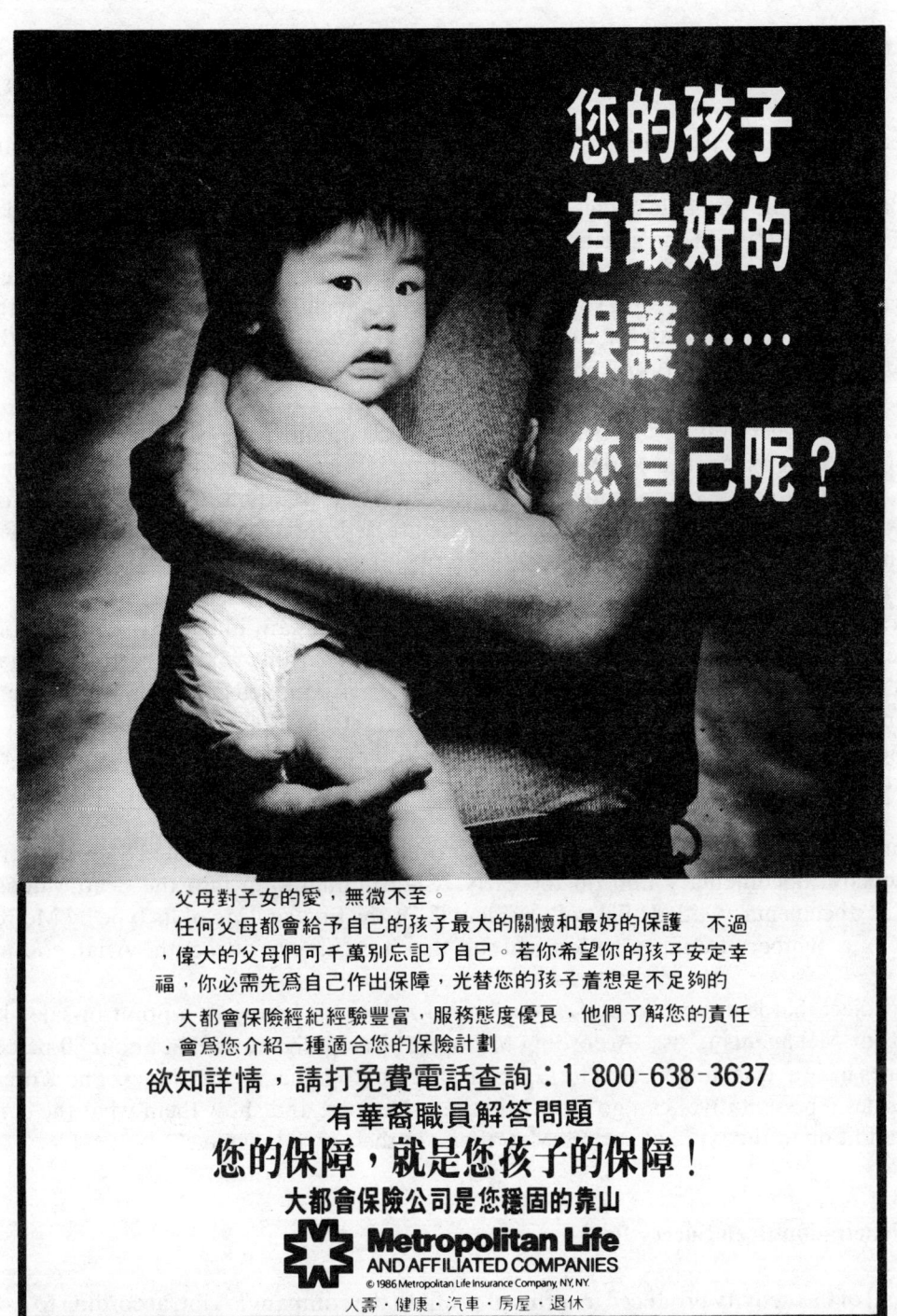

You Protect Your Baby. Who Protects You?

MET LIFE STANDS BY YOU.

Ad campaign for Metropolitan Life's insurance products, for the Chinese community (the same ad appears in Korean). Created by L3 Advertising, New York.

Asian communities, because "reality defines perception"—to gain consumer trust, a company must advertise. Companies that pursue consumers are perceived to be better, bigger, and more stable.

The advertising that Metropolitan is developing for the Asian market is directed toward giving information in a straightforward manner. Research suggests that humor is less effective in the Asian market than it is in the Hispanic and general markets. According to Lopez, "In the Asian market you have to be more careful. In the general market we find Snoopy amusing, and it's great because he doesn't offend anyone—but I don't believe it would work in the Asian community. Remember, Asian-Americans are looking for a solid, conservative financial institution, and I doubt that a dog would be a clever spokesman in this regard." The concepts that Met stresses in the Asian community are stability, tradition, family, and safety of principle.

Currently, all of Metropolitan's messages to the Asian community are being sent through the print media, using local newspapers to spread the word. "Print is the media of choice at this time," according to Lopez, "because of the complexities of language, dialect, and culture. It enables us to provide information in a widely accessible format. But there are definite plans to expand into television and radio in the future."

Although advertising is the most efficient way to present the company image to the public, community involvement is also an important and effective vehicle, especially when targeting ethnic groups. Although most of Metropolitan's community involvment is conducted through its public relations department, there are certain projects that stem from marketing. Metropolitan has donated time and money to organizations such as the Asian-American Voters Coalition, the Chinatown Development Planning Center, and the Chinese Kiwanis Club in Dallas.

In addition to becoming involved in Asian organizations throughout the United States, Metropolitan has developed a documentary film on the early Asian immigration into the Seattle international district. The documentary, titled "East of Occidental," is the first venture of its type by Metropolitan, and is one of a number of unique marketing tools that it is using to attract the Asian consumer.

Another project that is unique to Met, as well as to Asian marketing, is a point-of-sale video tape developed for Met agents to use. According to Lopez, "Research shows that about 80 percent of all Asian homes have at least one VCR. The tapes we have put together are in Chinese and Korean. With this tool, sales representatives can go into their clients' homes, and show them what the company is about, in addition to the types of sevices Met offers, in their own language."

Has the Penetration Been Successful?

What has all of this activity produced in terms of profit to the company? A lot, according to Lopez. The indicator of success is the increase in premiums. (Premiums are what clients pay for products and services.) In 1986, the typical premium increase for the insurance industry was, at the most, 5 percent. For Metropolitan in general it was 11 percent. In the Hispanic market for Met it was 15 percent. But in the Asian market the figure came in at 28 percent. The increase was huge, and one that Met is understandably proud of. According to Lopez, it all stems from the marketing effort. "I don't know any other company that is putting as much time and money into this market as Met is. Budgets for 1986 were nearing the million-dollar mark, and have increased by 40 percent in 1987. We consider this market as important as its Hispanic counterpart. It may be smaller, but in purchasing power and influence, it is equal if not greater."

In May 1987, Met took an additional step in targeting the Asian market. It moved one of its Asian reps into the home office to handle all Asian marketing. In a step similar to the move earlier by Lopez, Hong-I Chang has been appointed the new director of Asian marketing. Chang has been with Metropolitan for three years in the Richmond, Virginia area. According to Lopez, "Chang's appointment marks a major commitment on the part of Metropolitan to the Asian community. It marks the beginning of extensive efforts in targeting the Asian community."

Chang sees Met moving ahead in the area of recruitment advertising. Met has worked with this type of advertising, its ad featuring the tagline, "Make your first move to success!" The campaign, originally designed to bring in reps from the Chinese, Korean, and Hispanic segments, will now be used in attracting potential Filipino representatives, a new move on the part of Metropolitan.

For months, Met has been researching the Filipino market, which is expected to outnumber the Chinese segment in a few years. Currently, Metropolitan is using recruitment advertising as its first foray into this market. According to Lopez, "The best way to reach a particular ethnic group is through their own people. It is a tool that has proved successful for us in the past, with regard to the Hispanic, Chinese, and Korean groups."

In June 1987, Metropolitan began educator and product promotion advertising to the Filipino market, primarily via print, through such outlets as the *Philippine News*. For the most part, the Filipino population in the United States is a highly assimilated group. Immigrants tend to assimilate into American culture more quickly than other groups. But, according to Lopez, there is still the need to be addressed as Filipino, and to hear about issues that are unique to them.

One ad that will be used to address the Filipino market has already proved itself successful in targeting Chinese and Korean clients. The ad pictures a man holding a child, with the headline: "You protect your baby. Who protects you?" The ad appeals to this market, because it depicts people who are relatively young, combined with ideas about education and the protection of dependents. In addition, ads with the Snoopy spokesman will also be circulated in Filipino communities, which tends to be more open to humor in advertising than the other segments of the Asian market.

According to Chang, the movement into the Asian market will involve more placement of ads that promote recruitment and will highlight specific products that are popular in the group (such as Universal life, and L-93, a type of whole life insurance). In addition, two new television commercials for the Asian community will begin airing in the late summer or early fall of 1987. As Chang describes it, the spots will be 30 seconds long, one emphasizing sales, the other recruitment, and will be broadcast in Mandarin on Chinese and Korean cable stations.

THE JAPANESE MARKET

The Japanese community is just about the only Asian segment that Metropolitan has no plans to penetrate. Why? According to Lopez it's for two reasons. "First, a large percentage of the Japanese population in the United States has been here for a long time, and is for the most part fully assimilated, as well as bilingual. In addition, immigration from Japan has drastically decreased. Second, those Japanese who are coming to the United States now are here for only a short period of time. On the average about three years. They are here to do a job for their companies back in Japan, and then they will return. For the most part they are highly educated and speak English. It is not that we are avoiding this group, but we feel that our efforts would be more fruitful with the other groups. Our advertising to the Japanese is primarily in Japan."

CORPORATE COMMUNICATION

Metropolitan Life has done a great deal of advertising and marketing to both the Hispanic and Asian groups, but it has also done things other than mass-media advertising and community events to attract their numbers. One added attraction is a highly sophisticated telemarketing operation. On its 800-line systems, Met has employed Hispanic agents who are available to answer questions and provide assistance in contacting local-area representatives. As of yet, this service is not available in other languages, but telephone reps will assist Asian customers to sales offices with Asian personnel.

In addition, a direct mail campaign is being conducted throughout these ethnic markets. Letters are being sent to a million and a half Hispanics and a million Asians throughout the United States, providing information on Metropolitan's products and services.

THE HISPANIC AND ASIAN MARKETS

"Although the budget for these markets is only a small percentage of our overall advertising budget, it's significant in terms of cost and effectiveness," states Lopez. "We have found both markets to be very lucrative in providing good press. But more important, they have proved successful on the bottom line—in generating revenue."

For the most part the two groups have a great deal in common, a factor that has been a plus in targeting them. In general they show an enormous degree of loyalty to tradition, language, culture, and customs, in addition to being family-oriented and placing a high emphasis on education.

According to Lopez, marketing to this group is very successful when it is done right—which means doing your homework. "Before you get into it, know what you are doing. Study your market. Conduct focus groups. Obtain as much research as possible. And then, have the sales and support staff to back it up."

Lopez concludes by stating, "It's all well and good to do your homework and to understand the market, but being able to deliver what you promise is crucial. If you deliver, you will have loyal, repeat customers. If you don't, the effort will be counterproductive."

6

Understanding the Asian Market

THE DESIGNATION as "the nation's fastest growing minority" now rightly belongs to Asian-Americans. In 1970, the U.S. Bureau of the Census counted a mere 1.4 million persons of Asian descent. By 1980, the number had more than doubled, and then rose by 141 percent between 1980 and 1985. By 1990, the head count should stand at about 6.5 million; by 2000, one can expect about 10 million Asian-Americans.

Even with this rapid growth, Asian-Americans are very much a minority, and the 10 million projection translates into somewhat less than 5 percent of the total U.S. population. The groups are, however, concentrated in large metropolitan centers. One can predict that the size and dynamics of these "cities within cities" will become more prominent in the years ahead. (For projections on the Asian-American population in the year 2000, see Exhibit 6.1) Other trends in the making:

- *Chinese and Filipinos will be the largest ethnic groups.* Currently, the head count for both groups is roughly equal, and together they account for about 45 percent of the total Asian-American population. Filipino immigration rates are now edging upward; by 1990, Filipino-Americans may outnumber Chinese-Americans by a ratio of 10 to 8.5.
- *Slow growth for Japanese-Americans.* The current head count is just under 800,000 (about 20 percent of the Asian-American total), and will remain at this size—or increase slightly—in the years ahead. By 1990, less than one in ten Asian-Americans will be Japanese.
- *Family unification will continue to fuel immigration.* In years gone by, political upheaval (the fall of Saigon, for example) was the major force. The reversion of Hong Kong to Mainland

China aside, the major impetus for immigration will likely follow a different theme in the years ahead, as the recent arrivals from Southeast Asia use their foothold in the United States to bring family members and relatives to America. Vietnamese and "other Asians" may well continue as the fastest growing ethnic groups, almost doubling their numbers between 1990 and 2000.

The "foothold" or "family unification" phenomenon, regardless of ethnic group, has far-reaching resonance for marketers. The close family and community ties within all Asian groups means that current residents will carry the major (often exclusive) role of helping the new arrivals adjust to the new land. "Assimilation" includes choices of schools, living arrangements —and brand names. Thus, brand loyalty established with current residents can translate into new business with each new wave of immigration.

Exhibit 6.1. Projections of the Asian-American population—year 2000.

1980—total = 3.5 million

Chinese 23 percent
Filipino 23 percent
Japanese 21 percent
Asian-Indian 11 percent
Korean 10 percent
Vietnamese 7 percent
Other 4.8 percent

1990—total = 6.5 million

Chinese 19 percent
Filipino 22 percent
Japanese 13 percent
Asian-Indian 11 percent
Korean 13 percent
Vietnamese 13 percent
Other 11 percent

2000—Total = 9.8 million

Chinese 17 percent
Filipino 21 percent
Japanese 9 percent
Asian-Indian 10 percent
Korean 13 percent
Vietnamese 16 percent
Other 14 percent

Source: Robert W. Gardner, Bryant Robey, and Peter C. Smith, "Asian Americans: Growth, Change, and Diversity," Population Bulletin, Vol. 40, No. 4 (Population Reference Bureau, Inc.: Washington DC, 1985).

Understanding the Asian Market

DEMOGRAPHICS—SOME BROAD BRUSH STROKES

The dynamics of immigration and assimilation complicate the picture. For each ethnic group, the new arrivals have profiles different from longer term foreign-born residents, which in turn differ from second-generation Asian-Americans. For recently arrived Chinese (immigrated between 1975 and 1980), the median household had 3.9 persons. For the group as a whole, however, the family size came to 3.1 persons per Chinese household. Moreover, the number of persons classified as "managerial/professional" changes significantly with each category—new arrivals, foreign-born, or native-born.

This, in turn, affects income statistics. Widely publicized U.S. Census figures for 1980 disclosed that the median family income for virtually all Asian-American groups topped the national medians for other groups (including whites) by a significant margin. Often overlooked, however, was that the high numbers represented family income. Larger households (with more than one income-earner) accounted for most of the margin. (See Exhibit 6.2.)

Excluding difficulties with the moving target, here are some of the broad brush strokes.

- Significantly larger households, compared with both white and black U.S. populations. Exhibit 6.2 gives the medians for various Asian groups as a whole. For recent arrivals the medians would be higher—0.8 of a person higher for the Chinese and Filipinos, 1.4 persons higher for Koreans, 0.6 for those of Indian origin.
- More than one worker per household, and consequently higher per-household income.
- Higher high-school completion rates, compared with black, white, and Hispanic-Americans. With the exception of the Vietnamese, this is true for all major Asian groups. Consider, for example, males in the 25 to 29 age group. The Japanese are the highest, with 96 percent of the males completing high school. Koreans and Asian-Indians tie for second, with 94 percent of the males holding high-school diplomas. The Chinese come in at 90 percent, the Filipinos at 89 percent. (All of which top the white rate of 87 percent.)
- Even greater college participation rates. In 1980, 24 percent of whites, ages 20 to 24, were attending college. For Japanese-Americans of the same age, the rate was 48 percent; for Chinese, 60 percent; for Koreans, 40 percent.
- More professionals. For white Americans, the U.S. Census Bureau category of "managers, professionals, and executives" accounted for 24 percent of the population. The Japanese, Chinese, and Indian ethnic groups claim significantly higher percentages in this category, even with the generation variable referred to earlier.
- Urban living. More than 90 percent of all Asian-Americans live in urban areas—"standard metropolitan statistical areas," to use the Census term. More than half (56 percent) were in California and Hawaii.

A composite picture formed from the above gives some sense of the marketplace dynamics. Interestingly, very few U.S. companies have played to even the broadest of demographic features. For example, the large households and superior buying power make this a prime market for household goods and appliances. The educational dynamics and philosophy of upward mobility via education open the need for educational supports—be they encyclopedias or home-study guides. The reach for professionalism suggests a need for "image" products—be they suits, ties, or accessories. And so on. More of this later.

Exhibit 6.2. Median income and family size.

Ethnic group	Median Income Full-Time Worker	Median Income Per Household	Median Household size
Asian-Indian	$18,700	$24,990	2.9
Japanese	16,829	27,350	2.7
Chinese	15,753	22,560	3.1
Filipino	13,690	23,680	3.6
Korean	14,224	20,460 *	3.4
Vietnamese	11,641	12,840	4.4

*Line represents median income for white full time workers ($15,572) and income per household ($20,800). Average household size for white families was 2.7 in 1980.
Source: 1980 U.S. Census.

As with the Hispanic market, it's easy to say that the market isn't sufficiently researched. And as with the Hispanic market, the early winners will likely be those who shrug off this deficiency—forging ahead with research contracted to meet project needs. To get some sense of what can be done in the way of general and preliminary market analysis, we asked L3 Advertising Inc. to share with us previously unpublished data collected from two research projects.

CLOSE-UP ON THE METROPOLITAN NEW YORK CHINESE MARKET

It's a well-educated and affluent market—median household income in the $30,000 range. They're interested in quality products, but prefer to shop at Macy's rather than, say, Lord & Taylor, for a variety of reasons, including the former store's greater selection of merchandise and location. They're responsive to premium brand-name products in many product categories, but have yet to form brand consciousness or loyalty in others. They are responsive to advertising (especially television and radio), but rely heavily on word-of-mouth recommendations from friends in making product selections. Most own televisions, stereos, and VCRs. About half own washing machines and automobiles. Among those who do not own autos, half plan to purchase them in the near future.

These are some of the major findings emerging from L3's interviews of 411 Chinese respondents during the fall of 1986. The research methodology used a random sample technique, drawing primarily from Brooklyn, Queens, and Manhattan. Respondent demographics come close to matching national profiles in terms of education, family size, and professional status. The median household incomes, however, are slightly above those presented in the 1985 Census estimates.

As with any research project, the findings are representative only of the group under consideration—West Coast respondents may show different patterns on certain questions, such as car ownership and appliance purchases.

Still, the findings begin to create some map of the market. (Before going further, readers may wish to study the New York demographic profile on pages 83 to 96.) Let's look, first at buying habits and brand responsiveness, then at a second L3 study focused specifically on media influence.

Understanding the Asian Market

Note: Exhibits 6.3 through 6.17 are the property of L3 Advertising, Inc. 133 Canal Street, New York, NY 10002. Copyright 1986; all rights reserved. Used by special permission. The L3 agency wishes to note the contribution of May Leong, director of media and research, for her contribution to these studies.

Influences on the Buy Decision: Recommendations, Advertising, Brand Name

Who makes the final choice on a major purchase—the husband or the wife? As Exhibit 6.3 shows, it depends very much on the product, and responsibility may shift, depending on the product category. In a significant number of cases, husband and wife decide together. Rare is the situation in which the husband takes a unilateral lead in each and every major purchase—and even rarer, situations in which the wife alone makes all major purchases. In very few cases does the entire family sit down to talk about major purchases. One implication: research is needed on a product-by-product basis to position advertising and promotion to appeal to the decision-maker.

As with any homogeneous group, recommendations of friends and word-of-mouth experiences count heavily. As Exhibit 6.4 shows, 85 percent of the respondents cited word-of-mouth as a primary source of product information. Twenty-four percent indicated that they used *Consumer Reports* as an information source, a finding that reinforces other concerns with quality as a key influence. Forty-eight percent said advertising was important as an information source. Possible implications: post-sale service and customer follow-up to assure satisfaction may have important implications, in view of the importance of word-of-mouth experience. Advertising may well include components of product information; consumer education materials may yield high payoffs.

As Exhibit 6.5 reveals, respondents cited television as the most influential medium, followed by newspapers and magazines. Radio ads have less impact—but, one might add, far greater reach. Flyers, virtually none. These responses may, however, be somewhat misleading. In Hong Kong, television is clearly the medium of influence. Given the present state of Chinese-language television, respondents were likely answering more on the basis of past experience than current media consumption. (Additional research on how best to use various media will be presented in the next section.)

Logic says that brand name should be important in tipping the buy decision. All of the foregoing (the role of word-of-mouth advertising, the importance of personal experience with products, the reliance

Exhibit 6.3. The ultimate decision-maker when purchasing an item that costs more than $100.

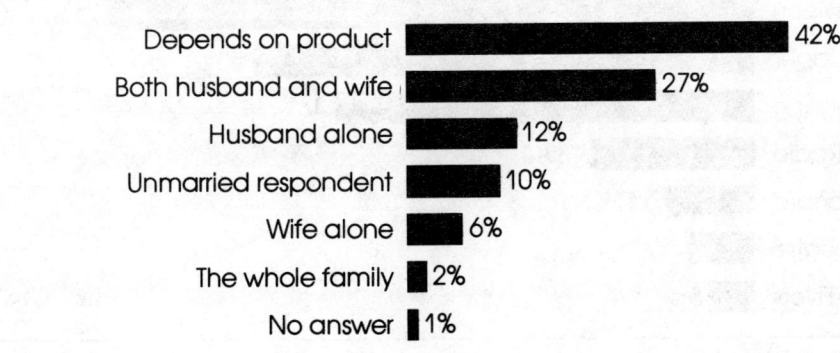

on *Consumer Reports,* the impact of television and radio promotion, and manufacturer's reputation for quality) underscore that importance. Interestingly, however, many respondents have yet to form their personal brand loyalties. Much of this may be a matter of cultural transition: In Hong Kong, recognition and loyalty are unquestionable, says Joseph Lam. But the transition to a land filled with a multitude of new and different brand names disrupts the loyalty, leading to new buying habits.

Asked, for example, to give "the first name of silverware that comes to mind," 89 percent of the respondents were unable to come up with any answer. The 11 percent that could name a brand were equally divided in citing four different manufacturers. Asked to give the first brand name of a china that comes to mind, 60 percent were unable to answer. Twenty percent cited names of Chinese manufacturers; 7 percent named Mikasa.

Exhibit 6.6 lists categories in which respondents said that brand was a key factor. Exhibit 6.7 shows responses to selected categories. In each case, the question was the same, "Off the top of your mind, name a brand of . . ." As with the silverware, many respondents were unable to cite a brand for the product category in question.

Exhibit 6.4. Sources of product information.

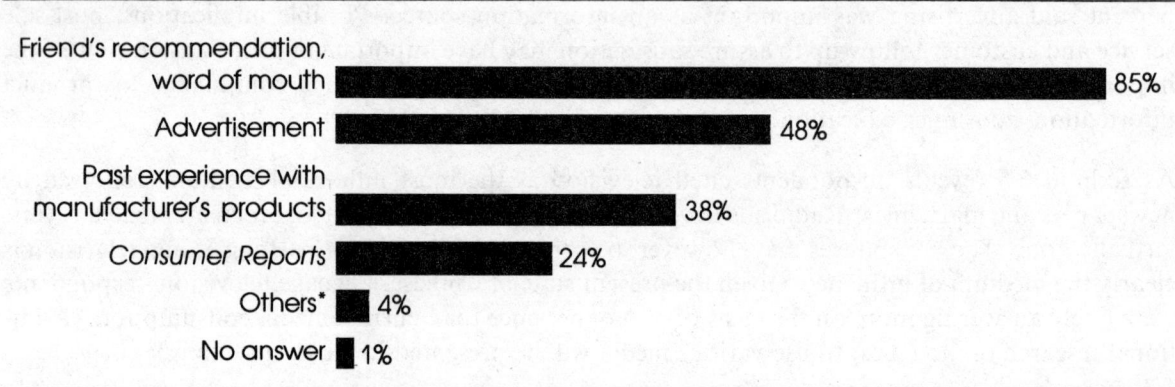

Total percentages do not add up to 100 because of multiple answers. N=411.

*Includes comparison shopping and catalogs.

Exhibit 6.5. The most influential advertising medium.

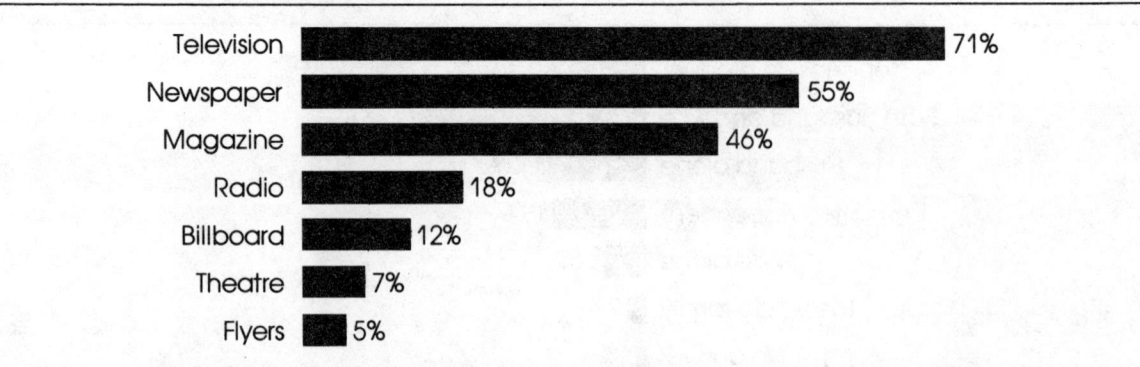

Total percentages do not add up to 100 because of multiple answers. N=411.

Exhibit 6.6. Product categories in which a brand name is important.

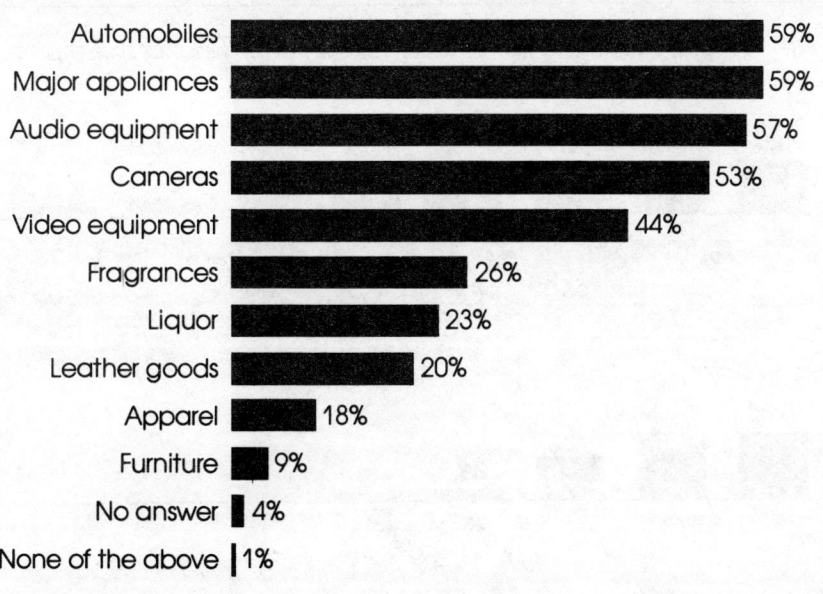

Total percentages do not add up to 100 because of multiple answers. N=411.

Note, however, that this brand-awareness test points clearly to product quality. It's Gucci in leather goods, Giorgio Armani in men's suits, Elizabeth Arden perfume. Asked to name an automobile, respondents are five times more likely to say "Porsche" than "Chevrolet."

Possible implications: campaigns designed to build brand awareness on the basis of prestige and quality may seed significant long-term benefits.

On the question of where to shop for apparel, there's no dispute. (See Exhibit 6.8.) Macy's is the hands-down choice, primarily because of the store's varied merchandise selection, partly because of the store's location. (One might argue that the respondents underrated location—because of the store's proximity to New York's Chinatown. Not true. Only 23 percent of the respondents were residents of Manhattan.) The concept of "selection" as a key factor meshes with the other findings. For quality-conscious individuals who have yet to develop clear brand loyalties, the opportunity to examine products from a variety of manufacturers makes infinite sense.

BUYING HABITS

Exhibits 6.9 through 6.15 provide insight into the market potential for products and services costing more than $200. Most of the charts are self-explanatory and deserve a close look by marketers interested in particular product categories.

As a point of departure, note that 61 percent of the respondents are apartment-dwellers; of these, more than half said that they intend to buy a home "soon." Half the respondents own automobiles; half don't. Of the latter group, about half plan to purchase an auto within a year. (Text continues, p. 95.)

Successful Marketing to U.S. Hispanics & Asians

Exhibit 6.7. "Top of mind" brand names.

Respondents were asked to name the first brand that came to mind for these product categories.

(N=270)

Automobiles

Porsche	Other	BMW	Toyota	Mercedes	Oldsmobile	Don't know	Rolls Royce	Ford	Chevrolet
19%	18%	16%	12%	7%	7%	7%	6%	4%	4%

Pens

Don't know	Parker	Cross	Other	DuPont	Sheaffer
37%	22%	20%	14%	4%	3%

Shoes

Don't know	Other	Bass	Italian made	Bally	Gucci	Nickel
50%	20%	9%	8%	7%	3%	3%

Leather goods

Don't know	Gucci	Other	Louis Vutton	Pierre Cardin	Italian-made
57%	17%	14%	7%	3%	2%

Liquor

Don't know	Remy Martin	Other	Johnny Walker	Courvoisier	Martell	Henessey
36%	17%	16%	12%	11%	4%	4%

Exhibit 6.7. "Top of mind" brand names. Continued

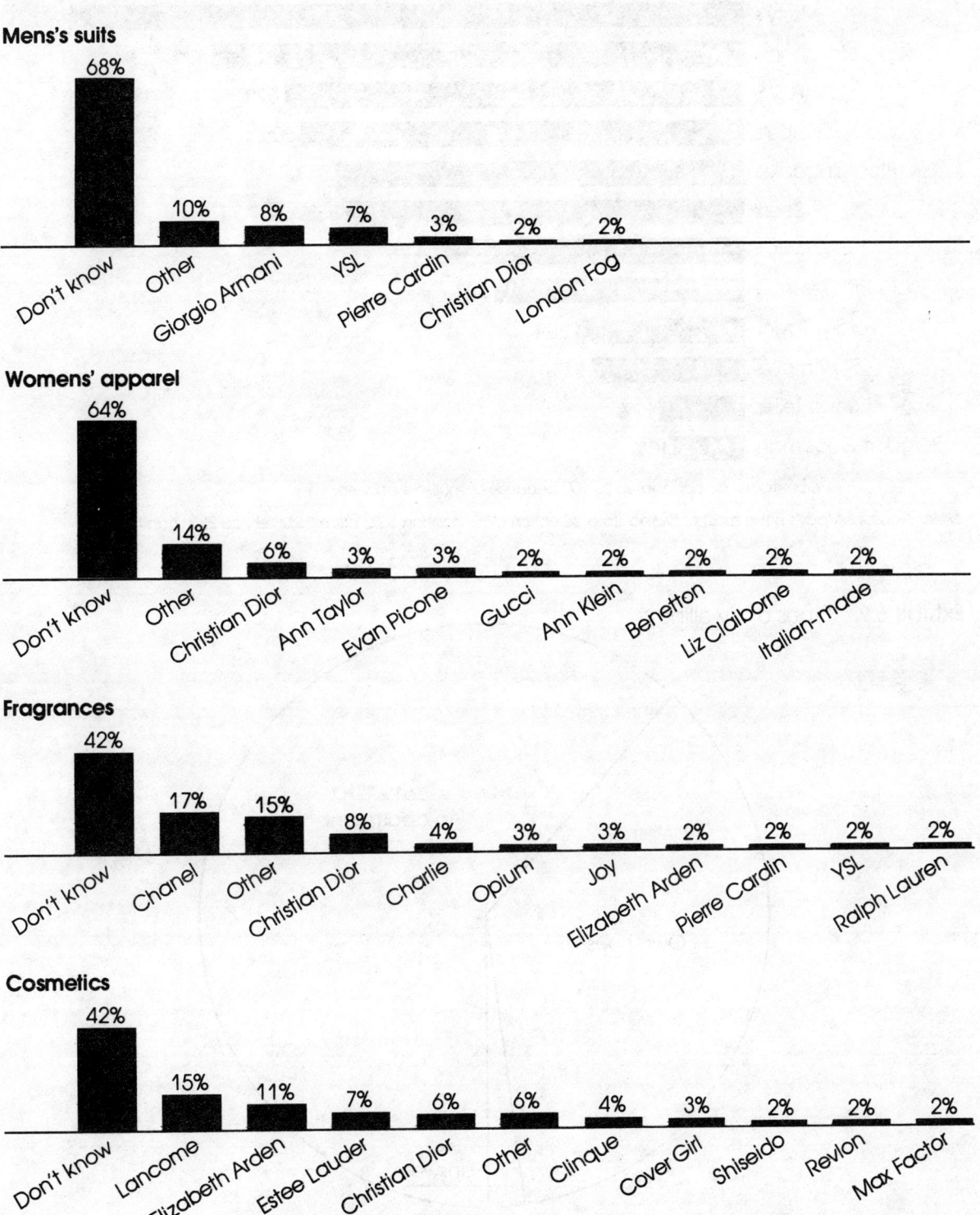

Exhibit 6.8. Retail stores in which purchases have been made.

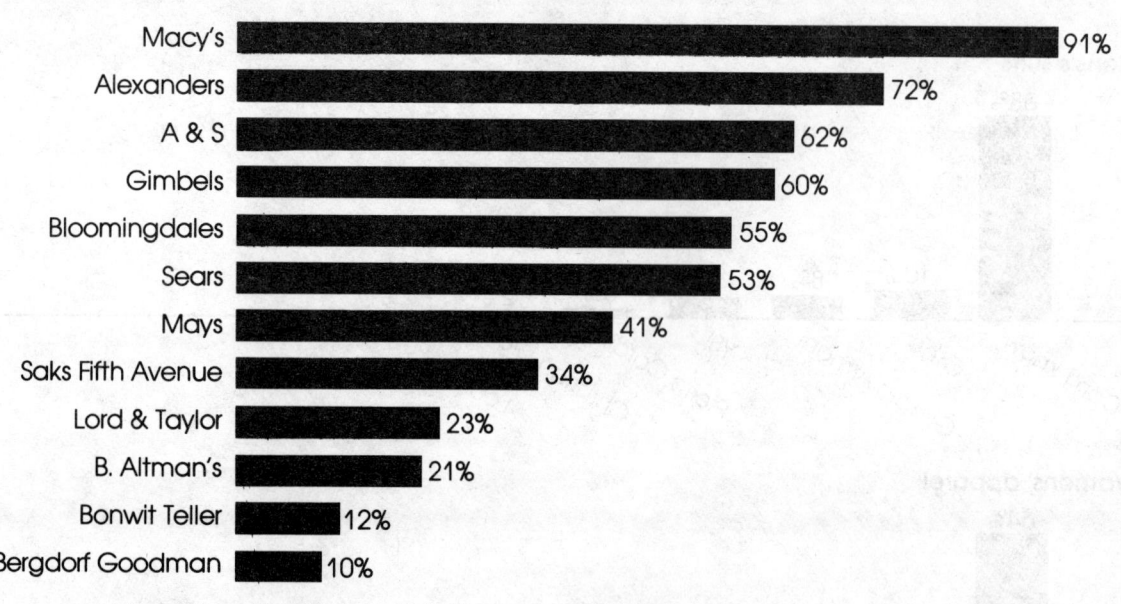

Percentages do not add up to 100 because of multiple answers.

Note: Reasons Macy's is the most preferred store: selection 69%; location 55%; price 25%; service 22%; habit 2%

Exhibit 6.9. Types of dwelling.

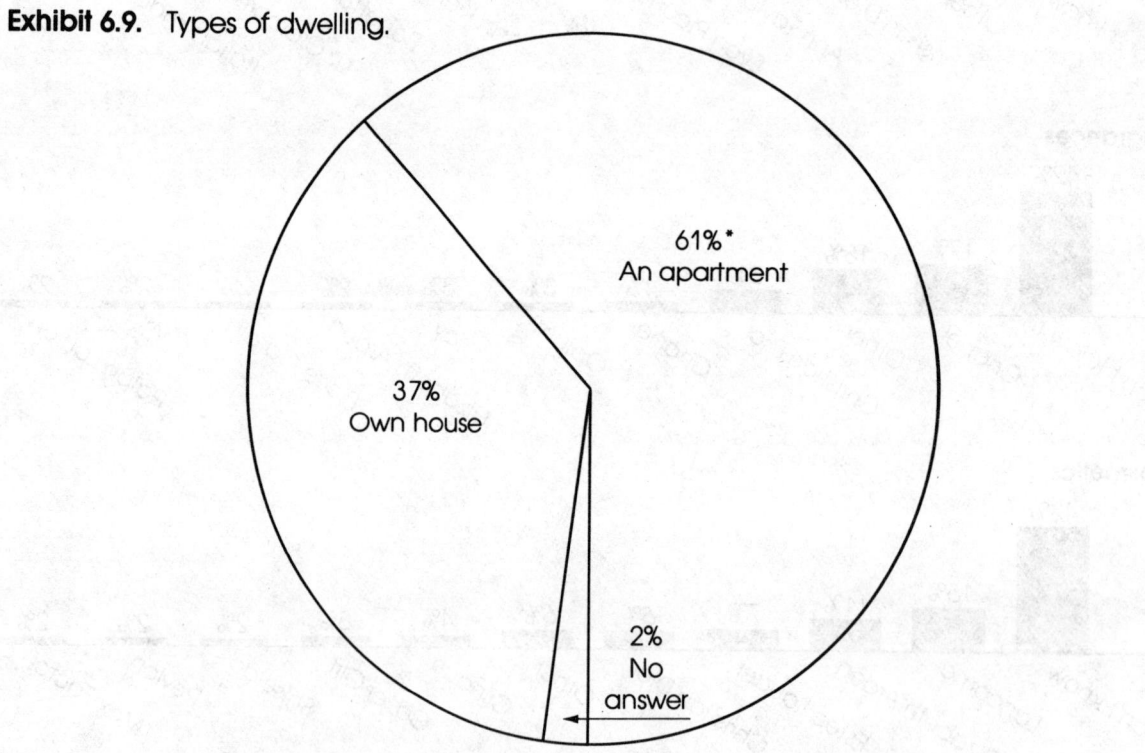

*For people who currently rent: 59% said they are planning to buy houses soon; 18% said they intend to buy a house at some point; another 18% said they don't know yet. Only 5% said no.

Exhibit 6.10. Car ownership.

Question: Do you currently own an automobile?

Yes 50%
No 50%

Of the 206 respondents who do own cars, 63 percent use their cars for both work and leisure. Thirty-two percent use their cars for leisure alone, while 5 percent use them strictly for work.

Of the 205 respondents who do not have cars now, 50 percent said they do not plan to buy one within one year. Forty-three percent said they will buy a car within one year, while 3 percent said maybe. Four percent did not answer the question.

Question: If you plan to purchase a car within the next year, will it be a new or used car?

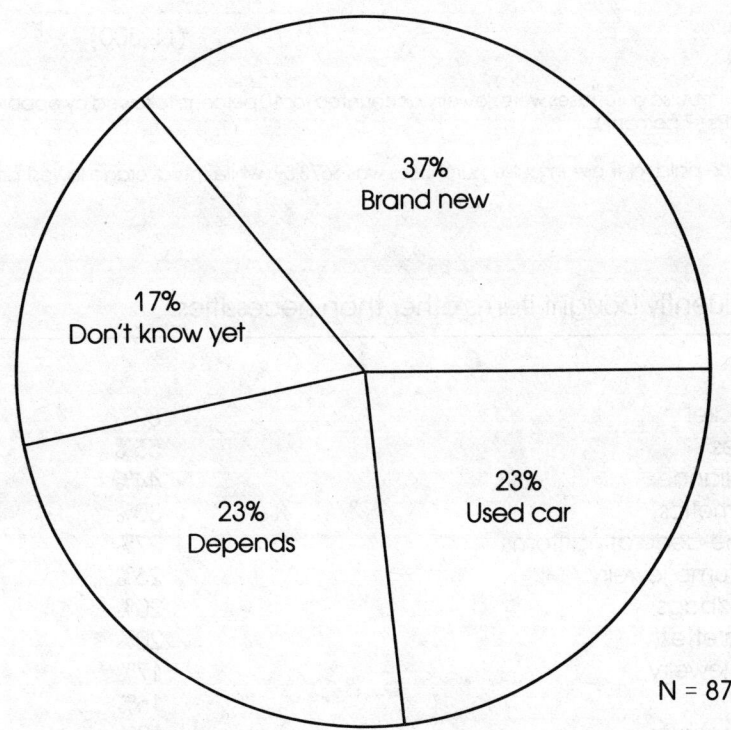

37% Brand new
17% Don't know yet
23% Depends
23% Used car
N = 87

Exhibit 6.11. Number of purchases over $200 made in the past six months.

One to three	49%
None	27%
Four to six	12%
More than six	12%

When asked what these items were, 25 percent of respondents said appliances (including air conditioners, washers, dryers, and other smaller appliances); 22 percent reported buying furniture; 21 percent said t.v.; 19 percent bought VCRs; and 19 percent bought apparel.

Number of the above purchases made by impulse.

None	56%
One to three	5%
Four to six	36%
More than six	1%
No answer	1%

(N=300)

When asked what these impulse purchases were, jewelry accounted for 10 percent; followed by apparel (9 percent); t.v./Hi-fi (8 percent each); and VCRs (7 percent).

The average highest price paid for these impulse purchases was $673.57, while the average lowest price was $246.43.

Exhibit 6.12. Frequently bought items other than necessities.

Apparel	82%
Shoes	55%
Appliance	44%
Cosmetics	30%
Home-decorating items	27%
Costume jewelry	26%
Handbags	20%
Cigarettes	20%
Fine jewelry	17%
Toys	16%
Collectibles	10%
Fragrances	10%
Liquor	9%
Books and magazines	6%
Others (including cassette tapes, arts & crafts, tools, cameras)	2%

Total percentages do not add up to 100 because of multiple answers. N=411.

Exhibit 6.13. Number of times friends are entertained both at home and in restaurants per month.

Only when there's an occasion	39%
Four times or more in a month	19%
Two to three times in a month	14%
Never	14%
Once in a month	12%
Depends	2%

N=411

Exhibit 6.14. Number of vacation trips taken in a year.

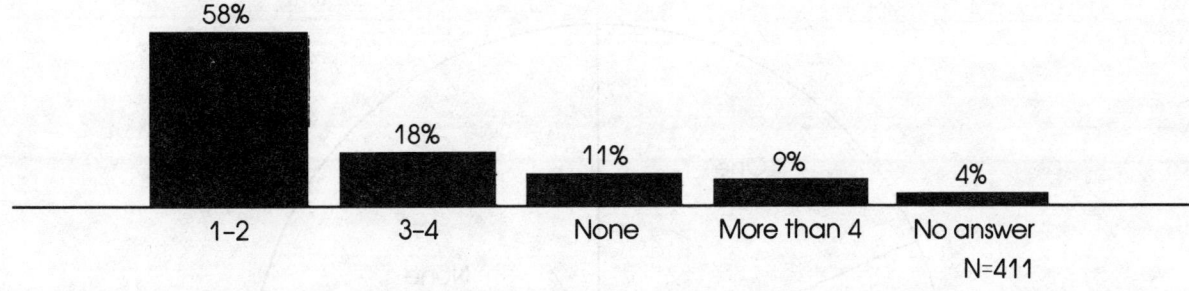

1-2	58%
3-4	18%
None	11%
More than 4	9%
No answer	4%

N=411

Planned vacation designations for this year.

Undecided	16%
West Coast	14%
Hong Kong	13%
Florida	10%
All others**	33%
No answer	20%

(N=366)

Total percentages do not add up to 100 because of multiple answers.
*Include Canada, Taiwan, Hawaii, Caribbean Islands, Europe, and other states of the United States.

Exhibit 6.15. This exhibit represents demographic information for 411 respondents (Exhibits 6.4 through 6.14).

Household size and income.

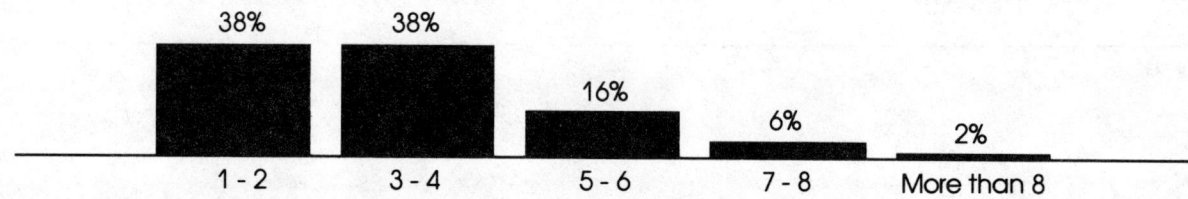

Number of people in household

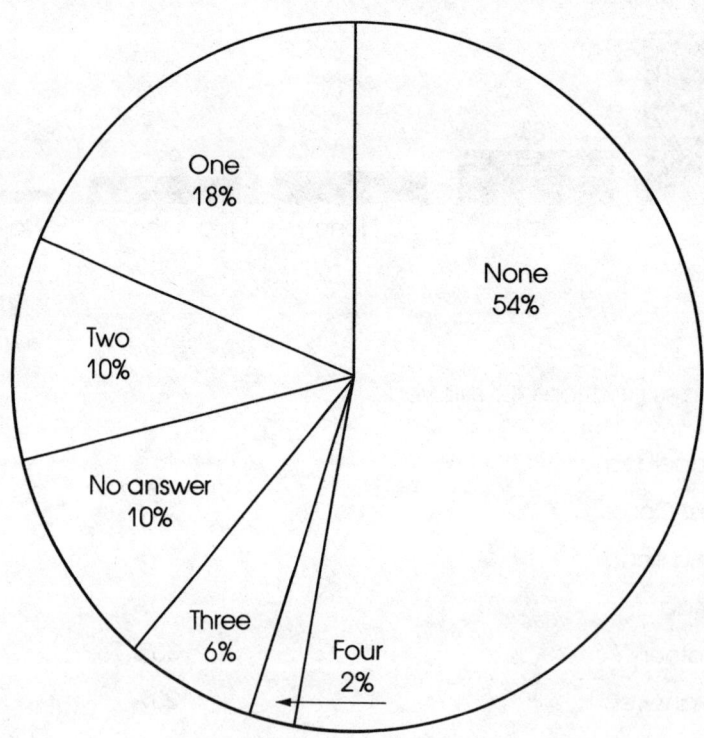

Number of children aged under 15 in household

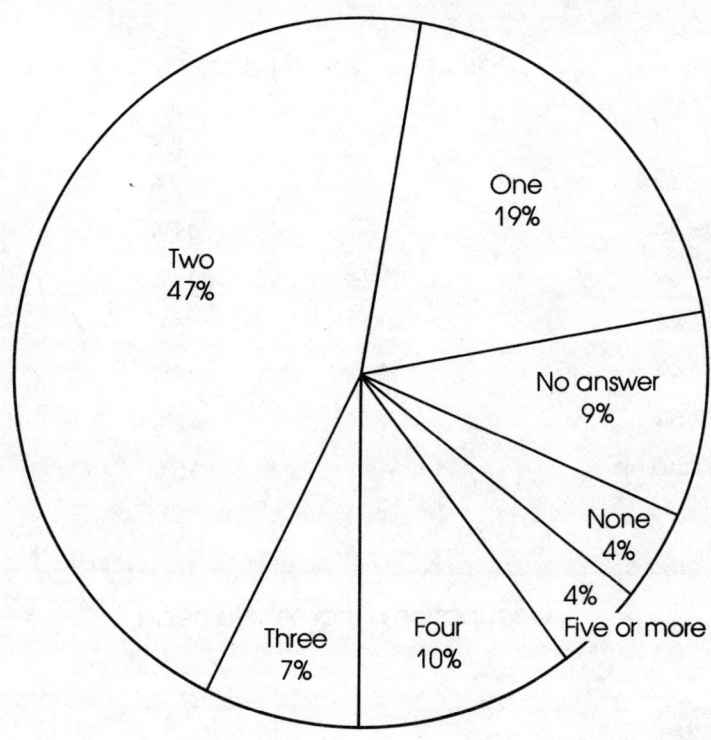

Number of full-or part-time job holders in family

- Two 47%
- One 19%
- No answer 9%
- None 4%
- Five or more 4%
- Four 10%
- Three 7%

Highest educational level of household head

Graduate school	31%
College	21%
High school	21%
Some college	9%
Some high school	7%
Few years of school	5%
Vocational/technical training	3%
Elementary school	1%
Never in school	1%
No answer	1%

Age of household head

20 - 24	4%
25 - 29	19%
30 - 34	19%
35 - 39	15%
40 - 44	6%
45 - 49	9%
50 - 54	12%
55 and up	15%

Occupation of household head

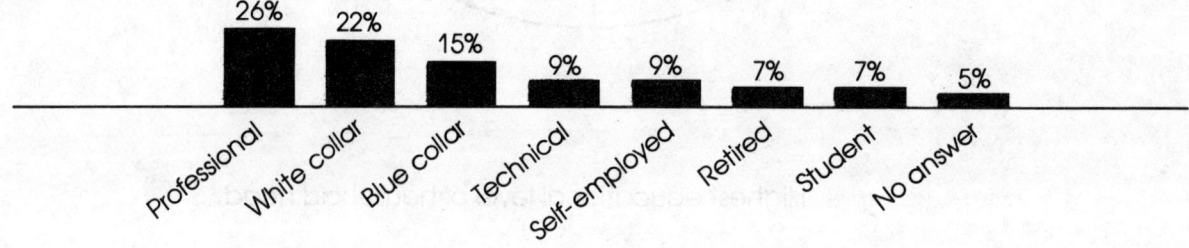

Professional	White collar	Blue collar	Technical	Self-employed	Retired	Student	No answer
26%	22%	15%	9%	9%	7%	7%	5%

Average annual household income

Under $10,000	12%
$10,000 - 20,000	23%
$20,000 - 30,000	18%
$30,000 - 40,000	15%
$40,000 - 50,000	7%
$50,000 - and up	18%
No answer	7%

Understanding the Asian Market

In short, the American dream (at least in terms of home and car ownership) is moving apace, undaunted by the urban landscape. The buying patterns are surprising, especially when we realize we're talking about New York residents—persons who have moved into a world of high-rise apartments, subways, and commuter trains. Part of the explanation relates to the psychology of immigration. The United States is still the land of opportunity, and home and auto ownership are tangible symbols of "having arrived." (This is, of course, true for any immigrant. Soviet engineers, for example, will often include an apartment floor plan as part of the first letter home—the fact of having acquired something so vast as a 20-foot living room being news of the greatest importance.) The other explanation stems, again, from the higher per-household income. Only 19 percent of the respondents were content to rely on the wages of one earner. About half were two-income households; the rest have more than two wage-earners.

All of this means a premium market for larger ticket purchases. As Exhibit 6.11 shows, about half of the respondents had purchased between one and three items costing more than $200 within the past six months. (Purchases included air conditioners, washers, furniture, televisions, and the like.) Respondents were then asked two additional questions: What was your highest priced purchase of more than $200? Your lowest priced purchase? The averages came out to $673 and $247, respectively.

In contrast, entertainment budgets may be somewhat lower than anticipated. Many entertain friends at home or in a restaurant "only when there's an occasion." The culture is important. Unlike the Hispanic community—where religious holidays and family traditions provide regular impetus for celebration—the Chinese are more reserved. Yes, events related to the birth of a child are important, and there is, of course, the grand New Year gala. But the causes for celebration come less frequently. Nor has the idea of frequent dinner guests and weekend entertainment caught on.

Vacations are a different story. About 90 percent of the respondents plan to take one or more vacations per year. Of those who had firm plans at the time of the survey, more than a third indicated trips that would involve air travel—to Florida, the West Coast, and Hong Kong.

THE LANGUAGE QUESTION

Do Chinese-Americans accept English-language advertising and identify with the message being presented? The answer for a majority, quite clearly, is no, according to a poll of the 333 respondents interviewed. Exhibit 6.16 shows why: first, note that it's not a matter of a language barrier as such. Only

Exhibit 6.16. Reasons for rejecting English ads.

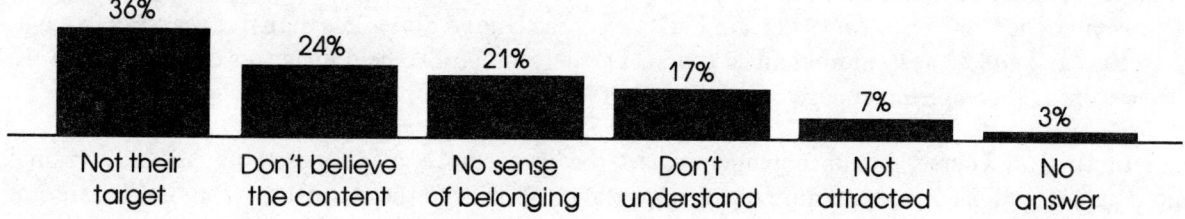

*Total percentages do not add up to 100% because of multiple answers.   (N = 171)

Exhibit 6.17. Influence of Chinese vs. English ads

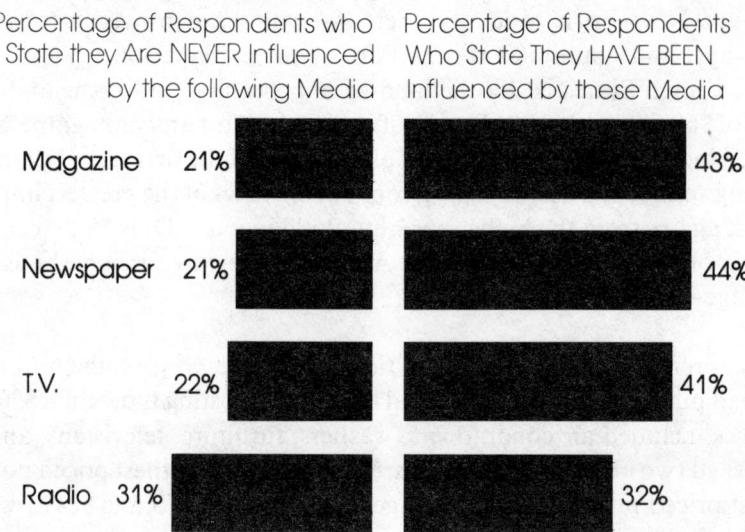

17 percent reject the English-language ads because they don't understand English. (Other questions indicated that about 90 percent of the respondents felt that they had at least a minimum competence in English.) Rather, it's a matter of identification. They feel that the ad is not for them. Three of the answers shown in Exhibit 6.16 are on this theme: "not their target," "no sense of belonging," and "not attracted."

One can approach the same question from another angle. Even if a person does not identify with an English-language ad, that ad may still exert an influence. A brand name sticks in the mind, sufficient interest is aroused to find out more, and the like. Following this line of reasoning, several additional questions were put to the respondents. Exhibit 6.17 shows the results. Slightly more than 20 percent deny that they have ever been influenced by magazine, newspaper, or television advertising in Englilsh. About 40 percent say that they have felt some influence. These are, of course, subjective answers—on the extremes. Between the two is a grey area—uncertainty—a significant number of respondents who couldn't honestly say whether or not the advertising had an impact.

Asked about their competence in reading English, 45 percent indicated that they could "get by," 31 percent described themselvs as "better than average" for Chinese-Americans, and 15 percent reported themselves as "below competence," "below average," or unable to write at all.

In spite of this competence with the intricacies of English, 86 percent stated that they regularly read Chinese-language newspapers. This percentage holds true regardless of how many years respondents had been in the United States (19 percent had been in the United States less than five years; 29 percent, 5 to 10 years; and the rest, more than 20 years). The percentage also held up across educational levels: 45 percent had completed college or graduate school; another 45 percent, high school.

All of this, of course, points convincingly to the importance of Chinese-language advertising: newspapers and magazines because of the importance of print to these consumers; radio, because of the reach; and—at some point in the future—television, because of the importance of this media in the homeland.

7

Players in the Asian Market

Again, a number of the respondents interviewed asked that we not disclose the names of their companies or details of their campaigns. As with the Hispanic market, much of what the respondents talked about is simply good marketing sense: a sensitive understanding of the market, use of key players who know the culture and language, qualitative and quantitative research, and the like. Among other reasons cited for entering the market:

1. *The fast-growing nature of the market.* Current statistics show that the Chinese market is growing at a rate significantly higher than that of the general population. As the current situation with Hong Kong and Mainland China comes to a head, the potential immigration of Chinese nationals to the United States could be tremendous.
2. *The up-scale and sophisticated nature of the Chinese immigrants.* Many Chinese immigrants were from the elite class in their native countries. They have chosen to come here to escape societies that no longer fit the way they want to live. Combine this with the first point—the anticipated immigration from Hong Kong—and you have a very large, up-scale audience primed and ready for your advertising message.
3. *The centralization of the Chinese community.* According to respondents this is a dream chance for any marketer. As with the Hispanic group Asian immigrants are usually found clustered in a few major districts across the United States. Even if they do not live in these areas, they are there on the average of once a week, either to visit friends or relatives or to do their shopping.
4. *The accessible and inexpensive nature of the media.* The primary media for advertising is print, more specifically newspapers. Advertising space in most Chinese-language newspapers is very inexpensive, easy to get, and seen by a significant number of readers.

Much of the research has focused on understanding the importance of the product or service within the target culture. When (on what occasions) is the product used? For what culturally related reasons is it used? How do important traditions and psychographics (respect for elders, the importance of childbirth) relate to the product or service? In some cases, the connections do not come easily. Life insurance, for example, is unknown in many Asian countries. A company can, however, appeal to the need for economic security and (because of the importance of education) savings for college education. Sensitivity to the culture feeds creativity in, for example, the use of important colors and images.

Again, respondents talked about support for the community and close involvement with civic and business groups. The relationships are more difficult to establish, and our respondents are holding their cards especially close to the vest in this regard.

HASCO: CONNECTING AT THE POINT-OF-SALE

For forty years, "baby's first picture" has come courtesy of Hasco International. Working in cooperation with 2200 hospitals in the U.S. and in six foreign countries, Hasco's baby photographers are on the scene to capture and develop baby portraits snapped in the first days, or even the first hours, of a newborn's life.

Increasingly, Hasco finds advantage in utilizing second-language point-of-sale "menus." According to Marc Arnold, Hasco's executive vice president for sales and marketing, instructions for ordering Hasco photographs have been translated into nearly fifty languages.

"We don't buy mass media advertising," Arnold explains. "We've seen a tremendously positive result from publishing standalone, self-supporting, full-blown four-color materials. We count on point-of-sale materials, with an emphasis on order forms and ordering information. The customer needs to understand how our program works and how to place an order.

"Historically, we've done these in English, with a separate black-and-white flyer in Spanish translation," Arnold reports. "Three years ago, we 'bit the bullet' and went to the expense of producing a four-color booklet in Spanish. The effort has been well rewarded. A segment of the Hispanic community is accustomed to being treated as a secondary market, and when the effort was made to treat them completely equally, the response was tremendous."

Why so? "Because it shows you've made an effort," says Arnold. "I think that's the most important thing: if that comes across, that you're solicitous and are making the effort, the foreign-language customer responds. Usually there's a high level of frustration. The foreign-language customer feels that the whole burden is on him. That mentality is not conducive to sales.

"The purpose of all our materials is communication. We bear that in mind as we arrange for translations into all these languages. Unfortunately, the numbers who speak other languages (neither English nor Spanish) don't really warrant the expense of a four-color piece, so we're left with black-and-white translations that go with the English materials."

Hasco's effort is not hit-or-miss. When a new hospital account is opened—cooperating hospitals receive a commission based on sales—Hasco surveys the hospital patient population. Finding a foreign-language group of just two or three percent of the local population calls forth a translation of instructions into the appropriate tongue. "We've moved away from a traditional order-form design to a menu approach," Arnold states. "People can look at a photo on the menu, see the price, and decide whether they want to buy it. We can get by with four-color menus in English, accompanied by instructional handouts in other languages."

Hasco sales representatives are sometimes armed with more than literature: foreign-language audio cassettes of the basic sales pitch. The cassette can be helpful in approaching potential Asian-language customers. "The cassette recorder may become standard equipment for our salespeople in the future," Arnold says.

Also, Hasco's Missouri-based customer support staff includes personnel fluent in foreign languages. "We've gone to some length to man our 800-line with Spanish-speaking people," Arnold reports. "That's an area I think many companies neglect. We've had Asians as well, but we've found them hard to recruit in our area. It's just very difficult when you get into the smaller minorities."

When those "smaller" minorities grow larger, Hasco will know of it from their salespeople. "I had a report of a tremendous influx of Vietnamese in Wichita," Arnold recalls. "The salespeople said it was tough to approach them. So we promptly obtained translations and support material.

"We don't find Japanese as a sole language," Arnold says in a review of language groups. "That's the issue—sole language—among the more recent immigrant populations or the insular communities where there is a full-blown internal community. That's a more specific question than trying to address everyone in their mother tongue."

Numbers, as always, are vital. Hasco has no current plans to produce four-color "menu" pieces in any Asian tongue, feeling that the black-and-white translations which accompany the English-language materials are working well. "I feel we're doing a good job in getting to the smaller populations," says Arnold. "I think we need to see a growth to something like 15 percent of the national population before it makes economic sense to produce a four-color piece in another language. I'm speaking now of the sole language, not a bilingual population.

"We're looking at a pyramid. When we think of opening the gates to the next level down, as we reduce to five percent, four percent, three percent—each time we knock it back a percentage point, we may be multiplying the number of language groups which qualify. If you're trying to keep twelve languages going, the problem becomes consistency. There's a logistical problem associated with keeping prices and services up-to-date in all your language pieces. The four-color piece doesn't have transient information in it. The accompanying translation avoids time-sensitive information."

Serving fifty different language groups, even if only with one-page insertions into the basic four-color booklet, works for Hasco at its point of sale. And where language is concerned, the babies don't seem to care at all.

KIKKOMAN/PACIFIC CHEMICAL: RUNNING IN REVERSE

To the second-language audience, stateside marketers play variations on a standard theme: present the product, establish brand identification and loyalty, bring the newcomers into the fold, and increase overall market share. Overseas corporations play the music in reverse. They follow the emigrating population to the States, carve out small sections in retail outlets, and then—perhaps—expand their customer base by inviting the native population to sample their "exotic" wares. Thus did the Kikkoman Corporation establish itself with its soy sauce, long a staple in Oriental diets but, 30 years ago, rarely found on American pantry shelves.

In plan and execution, the Kikkoman story is importantly different from the campaigns for Japanese electronic and automotive goods. From the outset, Honda, Sony and all that came with them or followed in their wake never expected their customers to be only Japanese expatriots or their decendants. Instead, they designed their campaigns for the wider American market.

But behind Kikkoman's success story lay a single role of the dice that brought a long-term payoff of $58 million in 1986 sales, and a market share of 50 percent.

Stirring the Sauce

Kikkoman's entry into American supermarkets built on its established presence in California and Hawaii. Local Chinese and Japanese ethnic grocers were pleased to carry Kikkoman's large, quart-sized bottles of soy sauce, because the only competitor, La Choy, packaged its product in 3-ounce bottles—"hardly enough for one meal," recalls Tom Yoshinaga, Kikkoman's national sales manager and a 30-year veteran with the Tokyo-based concern.

Two indicators prompted Kikkoman's move to a wider market. Caucasians were shopping at Japanese and Chinese grocers in increasing numbers, not only for oriental vegetables, but also for spices and sauces. And Chinese and Japanese restaurants were enjoying a new and expanding popularity. Today, with egg rolls sold in ball parks and sushi bars spawning in American cities, it is difficult to recall how exotic oriental food seemed to the American palate in the 50s. What became a tradition—Sunday night at the Chinese restaurant—was then an innovation.

Special labels designed for the American market were affixed to the product before it shipped from Japan. Tokyo was eager to handle the supply. The problem was demand.

"It was difficult to find a food broker to represent our line," Yoshinaga remembers. "We ended up with the smallest broker in all of northern California." The Theobard brokerage had one salesman, two shared reps, one secretary, and the boss. And if finding a broker was difficult, convincing wholesalers and chain stores to take the product was nearly impossible. A single account was all Kikkoman could boast after their initial efforts.

That changed, literally overnight—election night, 1958.

Kikkoman had a small annual ad budget—about $50,000—and an equally small agency, a two-man operation that funneled a tiny allocation to local Japanese newspapers ("Token advertising, just to support the papers," according to Yoshinaga). In mid-1958, adman Richard Guggenheim called Yoshinaga with an opportunity. San Francisco's Westinghouse television station, KPIX, a CBS affiliate, was seeking a single sponsor for its election night coverage. It was an all-or-nothing offer. The cost: $40,000—the entire amount left in Kikkoman's 1958 ad budget.

The decision was bucked up to the home office in Tokyo—which put it right back in Yoshinaga's lap. After an hour's consideration, he made the decision to put the whole bankroll down on the board.

Kikkoman had no filmed commercials; everything went out live. Local personalities were enlisted to read Guggenheim's copy and give endorsements. Every 15 minutes, from 6:00 p.m. to dawn's early light, the station updated the returns and Kikkoman presented its pitch.

The next morning, *Chronicle* columnist Herb Caen noted the impact with a pun on the name of a city councilman called Kiku. "I couldn't figure out who was running for office last night," Caen wrote. "Was it Kiku or Kikkoman?"

"Within 24 hours," Yoshinaga remembers warmly, "every account, every chain, every wholesale dealer who had turned us down called me, ready to buy. Within 24 hours we had one hundred percent distribution in northern California."

Everything had changed. Today, Kikkoman employs 54 people in its marketing division, and through the Saatchi & Saatchi/DFS agency's San Francisco office it spends $3 million annually in advertising. Sixty percent of the budget goes to television—with the commercials assuredly on tape or film, not live. Corporately, Kikkoman Corporation, Japan (the parent company) handles Japanese distribution for such American food suppliers as Del Monte, Ocean Spray, and Ragu sauces.

Kikkoman remembers its roots. It maintains a separate advertising budget for ethnic markets, which spent $100,000 in 1986. It buys time on Japanese-language broadcasts in San Francisco, Los Angeles, and New York, using a mix of commercials from Japan and domestically produced spots. It plays to the expanding Korean population with newspaper ads in that language and sponsors community events in ethnic neighborhoods. And following its traditional tactic, it places an expanding product line of soups and sauces in ethnic groceries and waits for evidence of a wider demand. "Crossover products cost money," Yoshinaga notes. "You need a very strong assurance that you can hang in with a modest budget. To launch a product today costs a minimum of a million dollars for distribution alone. On top of that, there has to be a media campaign. Our highly specialized products couldn't support that kind of budget." Nor does Yoshinaga envision larger dollar allocations for second-language marketing. "More and more ethnics are becoming bilingual," he says.

Pacific Overtures

Today, there is aborning a cosmetics and health foods concern that aspires to the same integration into the mainstream that Kikkoman has achieved. Pacific Chemical was founded in Seoul, Korea in 1945, in the wake of the Japanese defeat and the founding of the Republic of Korea. It develops and tests new products at its Pacific Beauty Academy in Seoul, which provides systematic training to both beginning and experienced beauticians. But Pacific Chemical has modern grail, half a world away: the counters at Saks Fifth Avenue, where it would compete directly with high-ticket American and European beauty aids.

In the United States, Pacific skin-care centers in Los Angeles and New York are a launching pad for the company's products, practitioners, and sales staff, and provide service to the women of the local Asian community—although an Occidental face is no rarity. Scan the shelves, and note the difference from other such establishments: the soaps, shampoos, rinses, balms, and powders are entirely Korean-made. From these centers, beauty "consultants" fan out for door-to-door sales calls, offering under the GG Cosmetics label 15 different kinds of soap, along with skin-care products, makeup, hair cleansers and conditioners, perfumes, and toiletries. From offices in Philadelphia, Chicago, and Miami, additional salespeople work the neighborhoods. Prices range from a low of $3.50 to a high of $50; the targeted customer is young (ages 14-25). For the professional trade, there is the Amos line of beauty products. Total U.S. sales in 1986: $3 million.

The key date for Pacific's worldwide marketing program is 1988. Enfranchised as an official sponsor of toiletries, household products, and foods for the 1988 Summer Olympic Games in Seoul, the company will put the Olympic identity to work on behalf of its line of health foods and drinks in a worldwide campaign. Ginseng Tea, already a popular item in health-food stores that reaches beyond the Korean population, will be matched with Oga-D, a natural herb drink, and Stevion, a pure natural sweetener.

The 1960 Olympic Games in Tokyo were an integral factor in a global "re-imaging" for the Japanese, from the exotic and delicate to the vigorous and ultramodern. Pacific Chemical is banking on the 1988 Games to help its Korean products become familiar and desirable. There are precedents; the plan may prove worth the price.

WHY DID THIS AD WORK SO WELL?

The Remy Martin ad on page 103 represents one of the most sensitive approaches to the Chinese market our researchers encountered. Every detail carries a wealth of information. The moon relates to the Moon Festival, an obscure celebration to Americans, but very important in Chinese culture. Traditionally a solitary event, the festival signifies a period of contemplation. The ad features fruits and cakes that are traditional elements of the celebration, while in the background a moonlit Brooklyn Bridge illustrates the blending of traditions—a bridge between East and West. More importantly, the ad implies, "We understand the Chinese heritage."

A perfect moon for a perfect cognac.

Ad campaign for Remy Martin cognac, highlighting the Chinese Moon Festival. Created by L3 Advertising, New York.

8

Asian-Language Media

AMONG THE Asian-language groups the Vietnamese are the odd folk out. They are younger, poorer, more recently arrived, and more crowded in their households. A lesser share of them have higher schooling or regular employment. Alone among Asian groups, their median family income is less than the median for all American families, and 30 percent of their families live below the poverty level—nearly three times the share of any other Asian group and almost nine times the share of Japanese-American families in poverty.

And yet this stricken people, cut off from their homeland (for the United States has no diplomatic relations with the People's Republic of Vietnam), shows a striving and an adaptability that may match and one day supersede the marks of the more settled groups. Census statistics show that more of their young men are enrolled in school than are Koreans or Filipinos of like age, and that more of their adult women are fluent in English than are Chinese or Korean women.

Most important, the Vietnamese-American community is growing rapidly. A population unmeasured in the 1970 U.S. Census and counted sixth among Asian groups in 1980, the Vietnamese had leapt to fourth by the end of 1985 and was projected to be third—larger than the Japanese or Korean populations—by 1990. By 2000, there will be a million and a half ethnic Vietnamese in the United States—more if restrictions imposed by both governments concerned are lifted and families can be rejoined.

"Many of the Vietnamese who come here are well educated but are not middle class. The skills they arrive with are not transferable," says Gary Wong of the Chinatown Local Development Corporation.

"This is not to imply that this is true of all Vietnamese. Many are firmly established in the middle class. But in global terms their percentage is not yet high enough to be considered a targetable market."

Nor can the population be reached via Chinese-language marketing. Vietnamese nationalism and French colonialism combined to separate the languages permanently and effectively. The very characters of the written language reflect the colonial influence. Whereas Japanese-, Chinese- and Korean-language ads feature Asian characters, Vietnamese ads use the Western alphabet to spell out the words phonetically, replete with French and Asian accent marks.

Vietnamese print media can be a hit-or-miss affair. Newspapers and magazines appear and disappear monthly. Where they exist, their circulations are very limited and entirely local. Four newspapers are published in San Diego alone—and circulated in San Diego alone. The Orange County *Vietnam Business Directory* (more information below) lists *34* incredibly diverse magazine titles, including the nationally distributed *An Ban,* the sports digest *Khoe Dep,* and *Nang,* whose masthead proclaims it "The Rightist Magazine Friday Edition for Women."

Other Vietnamese printed matter has issued from Los Angeles, San Francisco, Houston, and suburban Washington, D.C. AMA researchers have encountered unanswered phones, disconnected lines, and uncomprehending respondents in their efforts to trace many of these outlets.

DIRECTORIES AND NEWSPAPERS

In this transitory environment, the twin editions of the *Vietnam Business Directory* appear solidly established. Published by World Marketing Research, headquartered in Garden Grove, California, the latest directories (one for Los Angeles County, the other for Orange County) boast introductory "greetings" from President Reagan and California governor George Deukmejian. They are published in cooperation with the Vietnamese Chamber of Commerce in America—which, not coincidentally, shares a Garden Grove address with World Marketing Research.

To do good and to do well are certainly all-American aspirations. Luu Tran Kiem, president of the Vietnamese Chamber of Commerce in Orange County, proclaims them in his introduction to the 1987 edition of the directory:

"The freedom to choose a way of life to build upon the strength of an idea is the cornerstone of American small business and the secret of small business success. We have now in Southern California a vibrant Vietnamese community which is proud to work and contribute positively to this new homeland: more than 1,500 businesses are now owned and operated by Vietnamese. These businesses demonstrate our spirit of self-reliance and willingness to work hard, and constitute an eloquent proof of our commitment and dedication to the American free-enterprise system and the American way of life.

"We are very grateful for all the help and assistance we have received in our time of need. It is now our turn, indeed our duty, to return the favor and contribute to this country . . . [T]his *1987 Vietnam Business Directory* is an expression of this contribution. It is a tribute to the vitality of the Vietnamese business community and the American free-enterprise system."

Kiem's emphasis on small business is of a theme with the advertisers in the book. Only one national account appears: Coors beer, with a full-page ad. Another full page placed by the U.S. Postal Service outlines its available services. Local representatives of national accounts are present: Nissan, Buick, Subaru, and Porsche-Audi dealerships; Prudential, New York Life, and AllState agents. The majority of advertisers are Vietnamese businesses, joined by local merchants who serve the growing Vietnamese community. The result is a combination of business-to-business and consumer listings that carry to well over 300 pages.

While their yellow covers, thin newsprint, and directory layout give both editions of the *Vietnam Business Directory* the aspect of a classic "yellow pages," the Southern California publications make no use of that title. To the north, in the suburbs of San Francisco, a 232-page edition does boast the name of *Vietnamese Yellow Pages for Santa Clara County*. The San Francisco-based Direct Language Publishing, Inc., brought out its first edition in November 1986, with 2,700 business listings and a roster of advertisers, of which 72 percent are non-Asian-owned businesses.

Direct Language had prior experience in Asian-language directories. It published its first *Bay Area Asian Yellow Pages* in 1983, serving two language groups in the San Francisco-Oakland-San Jose region by combining Chinese and Japanese listings and advertising. Updated annually, and now distributed to 250,000 businesses and residents, the book has been a key factor in upping Direct Language's annual revenues from $550,000 in 1983 to nearly $4 million in 1986.

According to Direct Language president Jim Stein, it was far more difficult to publish the new Vietnamese book than the Chinese/Japanese yellow pages. The complexity of the Western alphabet, combined with the need for Asian notation meant "we had to proofread 17 or 18 times," Stein told the San Jose *Mercury-News*. That task done, the next was to compile a list of Santa Clara residents with Vietnamese surnames, to hand-distribute the book in Vietnamese neighborhoods, and to mail it to Vietnamese living in non-Vietnamese residential areas. First run: 22,000 copies—just a tenth of the circulation for the combined Chinese/Japanese product, but, thinks Stein, well worth the effort.

What reasons lay behind the popularity of such directories of second-language groups? "They show that business recognizes the group as a separate force in the community and sells to them alone," says Stein. The message is backed up by Stein's enlistment of advisory committees for each Asian-language endeavor. An April 1987 meeting of the Japanese Advisory Committee announced the inclusion of a map and a roster of San Francisco Japantown businesses, and an increase in the number of listings of nonprofit organizations in the next edition.

The Vietnamese directories and Direct Language's combined Chinese/Japanese yellow pages are local operations. Only one language group boasts a single nationwide directory: the *Korean Business Directory of the U.S.*, combining 16 localities from New York City to Fayetteville, North Carolina. It is, in a word, comprehensive. Its "blue pages" list everything from Broadway theaters and Greenwich Village jazz clubs to yardage and par for 100 notable golf courses (Augusta National to Wild Dunes). Fifty slick color pages offer a photographic tour of the United States, together with copy (all in Korean) about museums, historic sites, and economic centers. The back of the book sports maps and mileage charts. And, finally, there are nearly 1,100 pages of listings, the subject headings in Korean, the business names in Korean and English, and the street addresses and phone numbers in English.

The advertisers are themselves Korean: travel agents, trading companies, restaurant suppliers, real estate dealers and developers. And, in full color on cover three, Korean Air Lines, offers its "prestige class" to Korean travelers. KAL is the directory's sole example of what might be termed a "national account."

But national accounts are neither the pursued nor the pursuers among Asian print media. "Why would we have American advertising?" a representative of a Korean newspaper asked an AMA researcher. "We are Korean!" Another voiced suspicion: "Americans are interested in those of us who are economically established, because we have money to invest in their businesses—especially real estate." (A quick review of Asian-language print advertising confirmed that a large portion of advertisers are indeed real estate agencies.) The same source took pride in Korean *resistance* to assimilation. "You have to admire the way they [Koreans] are able to hold onto their homeland in this country," he said. "They haven't given in to American pressure like the majority of immigrants. We must be a very strong-willed people."

The attitude is not universal. Kyung J. Kim, publisher of the *Korean Independent Monitor*, thinks it "unfortunate" that he has no American advertisers. "I am currently developing a project on how to acquire American advertisers such as lawyers, doctors, higher education institutions, suppliers for Korean grocery stores and of dry cleaning machines," says Kim. "I don't have a set plan, but I imagine I will compose a letter explaining my paper and the benefits of advertising in it, along with a table of prices." Current rates: $500 for a full-page insert, $300 for a half-page.

Kim can count little on home support from Korea; editorially, the *Independent Monitor* is critical of the Korean establishment and carries heavy coverage of the opposition. Claiming a nationwide circulation of 82,000, Kim prints two-thirds of his editorial copy in Korean, one-third in English.

"Most of our readers are first generation, and we have to teach them the new reality of the second generation and how to be more flexible toward them," he says. "We also have to help the second generation to promote itself in this country. In the future I hope to see the English-language portion of our paper larger than the Korean portion."

Older than Kim's *Independent Monitor*, with a claimed circulation of 15,000, is the *Korean Times*, celebrating its twentieth anniversary in 1987. The *Times* is published daily in Korean, twice a week in English; the English edition carries essays by Korean students. Managing editor Pok Lin Choi says his primary advertisers, too, are real estate agents. "Agencies come to us to ask if they can buy space," Choi reports. "They know the Korean market is big."

Korean restaurants, local banks, and import/export firms are the old reliables for the *Korean Sunday Times* of New York (circulation: 20,000) and Los Angeles (15,000). Both publish political and economic news of Korea and the United States, both find half their circulation among subscribers, half from newsstand sales. The Los Angeles-based *Korea Today*, in its first year, specializes in law, medicine, health, and education coverage, and won't give out circulation figures or ad rates "because of competition." In contrast, the *Korea News* circulates a printed rate sheet and allows inserts to be charged to MasterCard, Visa, or American Express. A full-page in its daily editions costs $1,200 and reaches a claimed 18,000 readers with both English and Korean editorial content.

The *Chosun Daily News* is the American daughter of Korea's largest daily, the *Chosun Ilbo*, and claims to be "the fastest growing Korean newspaper in this country." It states its daily American circulation at 10,000 to 12,000. Its rates, which include a free translation service, start at $900 for a full-page unit, with frequency discounts up to 20 percent. A close competitor in both Korea and the States is the *Dong-A Daily News*, which began American publication 15 years ago and now boasts a circulation of over 100,000 in the tri-state New York area. "Readership consists of well-established professionals," says editor Shoon Shim. Like the *Chosun Daily News*, the *Dong-A Daily News* takes day-old editorial matter from its Korean-based parent and supplements it with local (New York) material, and publishes about 20 pages a day, entirely in Korean.

"We treat advertising as a science," Editor Shim explains. "It doesn't simply convey information; it also performs an education role to provide the standard of values with which the consumers may judge their society and the people around them." *Dong-A*'s consumers include "political, social, educational, cultural, scientific, and sports leaders, as well as middle-class citizens. The balanced distribution of readers appeals to advertisers."

"We take it on ourselves to be a means of self-expression for the Korean people," Shim states. "We advocate democracy. We stand for cultural enlightenment." *Dong-A*'s exclusive reproduction contracts with the *New York Times* and the *Times* and *Sunday Times* of London speak to its commitment to be the "newspaper of record" for Korean readers.

Dong-A's list of advertisers reflects the "establishment" nature of the paper: four major insurers—Equitable, Metropolitan Life, New York Life, and Prudential—appear in Korean-language ads, along with three airlines: Northwest Orient, Japan Air Lines, and, of course, Korean Air Lines. Two major New York construction firms, the Harry Macklowe Organization and Wong Construction, also take space. But according to advertising executive Young Kim, consumer-goods marketers have yet to break the barrier. Instead, the familiar list of import/export firms, restaurants, and real estate agencies supply the advertising dollars.

The story is much the same with Chinese and Japanese print. The Chinese-language *World Journal* is distributed in "all the major cities," according to account executive Caroline Lo, and again it is insurance companies and airlines that provide the only national-account penetration. The paper, which publishes East and West Coast editions, runs color on its front and back pages, black and white in between. The paper can translate English-language ads or aid in the preparation of new material.

Chinese holidays provide a key entry for advertisers, says Ms. Lo: the Moon Festival; the Dragon Boat Festival that runs from late May to early July; the Chinese Fathers' Day on August 8; and, of course, February's Chinese New Year. Half the back page in either the eastern or western edition will cost an advertiser $1,200, a full inside page slightly more ($1,340).

Still, the newest, slickest, and most upbeat vehicle to reach Asian-American consumers, and the one with the greatest display of consumer advertising (including Dunhill cigarettes, Maxxum cameras, Ralph Lauren's Chaps cologne, and Bally shoes), is published entirely in English. *AsiAm*, an Asian-American magazine, claims 75,000 monthly readers, 78 percent of them of Asian descent, with an average household income of $67,000.

"Our market is responsible for buying over 10 percent of all luxury items nationally, and in excess of 30 percent of such goods in the Los Angeles area . . . [R]each an overlooked consumer group with an unprecedented tradition of product loyalty, and an income level 40 percent higher than the national average," reads *AsiAm*'s fact sheet. The underlying claim is the same one that deflects most advertisers from Asian-language advertising in the United States: the consumers whom advertisers want are best reached via mainstream routes, with their signposts in English.

The *U.S.-Japan Business News*, a weekly headquartered in Los Angeles, carries a rare mixture of advertising. In the same tabloid-sized 36-page issue, one may find full-page ads in English (Canon copiers, Nissan automobiles), Japanese (Panasonic audio/video systems), and both languages (NEC microcomputers). There are American (read international) firms advertising in Japanese (Arthur Andersen & Co., Universal Business Interiors) and Japanese manufacturers advertising in English (Mazda, Mitsubishi, Toshiba). The editorial content is presented entirely in Japanese—and in early 1987 that content included a Japanese translation of *The Reckoning*, David Halberstam's popular study of U.S. and Japanese automotive firms.

The *U.S.-Japan Business News* claims a U.S. circulation of 35,000; its reader profile indicates a median household income of $45,000, a 95 percent college-graduate level, a 76 percent professional and business occupational listing. A single full-page black-and-white insert goes for $1,600; color capacity allows for a $3,000 cover four-color insert. There are discounts for multiple placements.

More typical of domestic print media is the *Hokubei Mainichi*, a full-sized San Francisco daily (Tuesday through Saturday) printed in both English and Japanese. Such dual-language presentation is aided by culture: the front page of a Japanese newspaper is the back page of an American one, and the *Hokubei Mainichi* works toward the middle, its English-language advertising covering English editorial (with inserts from the California First Bank and the Sumitomo Bank of California) and Japanese consumer and travel ads dotting the Japanese editorial.

Its monthly rates for daily insertions vary with the language employed: a two-column 4-inch ad costs $450 in the English section, $385 in the Japanese. One-time insertions run $1,200 for a full page in either language. The ads reach an average circulation of 8,500, described by the advertising department as "either Japanese-Americans or Japanese who currently reside in the United States." The paper, which will celebrate its fortieth anniversary this year, focuses on local events—marriage announcements, museum exhibits, and community festival news dot a typical (English-language) front page.

The coverage offered by the *Kashu Mainichi*, or *California Daily News*, casts a wider net. Seven front-page stories in English are datelined Tokyo, along with a "News Briefs" double-column with four Tokyo datelines. A masthead box lists the daily yen-dollar exchange rate. Like the *Hokubei Mainichi*, the *Kashu Mainichi* publishes five times a week, out of Los Angeles; like its San Francisco rival, its Japanese-language advertisers tend to be trading companies, restaurants, and home service providers. Its circulation is also similar: 7,000.

The small numbers speak to the central point: advertisers may reach the upwardly mobile Japanese-American market via mainstream advertising or, its publishers hope, such targeted English-language vehicles as *AsiAm*. Guided by market and motivational research, advertisers—especially of consumer goods—find Hispanic-Americans and Japanese-Americans to be very different cases. The conventional wisdom is that the former are heavily influenced in matters of brand loyalty by Spanish-language electronic and print messages; the latter, hardly at all by Japanese-language domestic marketing. Certain advertisers do find it worthwhile to place Japanese-language ads in the United States; the target there is the affluent Japanese managerial class, stationed stateside for a period of three to five years in what remains an important career step in Japanese companies.

ASIAN TV/RADIO

"The more micro the communication channel, the better." That overview from AT&T's national marketing manager, Al Binford, poses the question: "How micro is micro?"

In March 1987, Korean American Television solicited advertisers with a boast(?) of 1,500 daily viewers in the Los Angeles area. "Four to five new viewers are getting KATV each day," their letter read. "That shows almost 10 percent increasing rates each month."

Indeed. But taking KATV's minimum buy—$1,000 monthly for a daily 20-second spot in the 6:00 to 7:00 p.m. slot—adds up to a $22 cost per thousand (CPM), assuming that all cable-wired homes are tuned in. The rationale for a buy at that price and level of penetration: KATV is the only game in town.

But it is not. It is second in the market, attempting to steal a share of the far larger audience established by Korean TV Enterprises, which broadcasts over UHF Channel 18 in Los Angeles. As a broadcast station, it is available without cable to the entire Korean population of Southern California, currently estimated at 400,000. Channel 18's Korean-language programming, aired daily from 8:30 to 11:30 p.m., claims to reach half of that audience. Its rates: $300 for a 30-second spot, for a CPM (for 200,000 viewers) of $1.50.

No question but that the business of t.v. advertising to California's ethnic Koreans has wide margins. No wonder, either, that local restaurants and variety stores are the primary advertisers, with a foray by a local Cheverolet dealership added on. Why would any advertiser buy KATV at $22 CPM rather than Channel 18's Korean audience at $1.50? The obvious answer, as true in Korean-American households as anywhere else: cable-wired homes house more affluent consumers.

Korean TV Enterprises' Channel 18's programming is entirely in Korean; KATV integrates an English-language talk show for the bilingual second generation and American movies subtitled in Korean. Its drama ("Terms of Love," "Love and Ambition," "Desire") and variety ("Pop Song") are bought from Korea's one major network, KBS. Both stations run news and sports programs, with emphasis on news from the Korean peninsula. In this regard, they are in a position to counterbalance the heavily pro-government stance taken by most Korean newspapers.

The split between wired homes and airwave transmission is apparent in the New York metropolitan area as well. The newly inaugurated Korean channel claims a viewership of 3,000 households, which pay $25 a month over and above their basic cable charge for access to 12 daily hours of Korean talk shows, movies, and sports. Six minutes of every hour is commercial time; an advertiser's $1,500 per month garners 60 spots. The Korean channel's estimated cost per household—and all these figures can be only estimates, as no Nielsen or Arbitron numbers are available—comes to $4.15.

In competition with the cable outlet is Daehan Broadcasting, which via the airwaves captures an estimated 150,000 viewers on UHF Channel 47. The seven-year-old broadcasting firm sells 30 seconds of its Sunday morning programming for $350, for an estimated CPM of $2.33. Again, restaurants and stores are the primary buyers of time, with additional contributions from Korean Air Lines and New York's Dollar Dry Dock Savings Bank.

Above the commercial fray stands Korean Educational Broadcasting, a nonprofit firm that sends an hour a day of Korean programming over New York's UHF Channel 25. English lessons are part of the mix, as is local news, business information, and instructional programs about U.S. tax and immigration law. No ads are accepted.

Ads that run on the commercial stations had better stand out: 15 percent of Daehan's broadcast time is dedicated to paid spots. Moreover, Korean channels tend to run commercials in a large block of time, rather than interrupt programming for two minutes in the American fashion. "Korean t.v. runs commericals before and after a drama, not during," says Woojin Kim, a sales representative for the Korean channel.

There are other important factors at play in the programming, according to Kim. "In Korea the government controls the t.v. stations, so the programs can't say anything bad about the government or make fun of government officials," he reports. Perhaps as a result, the number of comedies available is severely limited, and heavily dramatic soap operas fill the time.

Radio, not television, carries the oldest Korean-American broadcasting concern, and the one with the most widespread audience. KABC, which began broadcasting 15 years ago, today sends its signal to Los Angeles and to four cities along the eastern seaboard, and added Chicago on June 1, 1987. A subcarrier FM station, KABC leases its frequency from the National Broadcasting Company, which bases its rental fees on the size of the audience. In turn, individual subscribers buy or lease special plug-in adapters that permit their radios to receive the signal. KABC claimed 22,000 nationwide subscribers in Los Angeles, Philadelphia, Baltimore, Washington, and New York before adding the Chicago market to its activities. In New York, its signal originates out of a broadcast center in suburban Queens. The network signal dominates affiliate programming, but locals can and do insert news slots.

KABC made a major leap forward in 1984, expanding from a once-a-week broadcast schedule to a daily, around-the-clock operation. The programming split is not so very different from that of a typical broadcast operation, though with perhaps more emphasis on news. Public-affairs programming takes up 25 percent of the air time, in line with KABC's strategy of "educating the second generation." Of the rest, 50 percent is music-oriented—traditional Korean sounds as well as modern pop—and another 25 percent is devoted to drama. All of it is in Korean.

KABC vice president Hojin Lee estimates that commercials fill 8 percent of the broadcast time, much of it shared with local affiliates. Multiple network spots cost $200 for a week-long insert; rates are negotiable. Major advertisers are Korean wholesalers and local restaurants. "We're not really interested in American advertisers," says Lee. "Advertisers come to us."

Mark Okrausky, the manager of technical operations at NBC's WYNY-FM in New York and overseer of the leasing operation, calls the subservice "an inexpensive route for ethnic groups to deliver programming to their audience." KABC holds a ten-year lease, and pays "less than six figures" for the privilege, according to Okrasuky.

In strong contrast to the busy activity in Korean-language broadcasting, there is the steady presence of the World Television Corporation (WTV), which supplies five hours of Chinese-language programming every week to an estimated 600,000 Chinese in the New York metropolitan area. Three hours go out over WNYC-TV, New York's municipal television station, and two hours—Saturday nights from 6 p.m. to 8 p.m.—are leased from Channel 25, the carrier for Korean Educational Television.

On this latter station, game shows, soap operas, and variety entertainment purchased from Taiwan and Hong Kong combine with the locally produced "Life Style in New York" program. This builds around an interview format to deliver information on investments, health care, consumer education, and new technologies. The ten-minute segment plays at 6:20 p.m. on Saturdays and is a key to World Television's stated objectives:

- To enable WTV's commercial clients to build a better image and to expand their businesses;

- To help WTV's viewers gain interesting and important knowledge, such as guides to buying a house or car, to investing, to learning skills, and to eating and exercising well.

Unlike the Korean broadcasters, World Television offers specific viewer demographics to potential advertisers. These figures show a predominantly female audience (54.4 percent). Further breakdowns are offered, by age (the 25 to 49 sector predominates, at 60.2 percent), and by occupation (working people, 38.6 percent, housewives, 25.1 percent). To reach them, WTV charges one-time rates from $120 for a 15-second spot to $620 for a full two minutes. All rates are subject to multiple-spot discounts and rebates, and production charges are included; agency fees are not.

As it begins to expand its two-year broadcast operation, World Television plans to establish a West Coast presence and begin radio operations. With groundwork laid by their print activities and bookstore operations described elsewhere, World is in a strong posture for growth.

In a familiar competition, a cable-based station goes against World's broadcast signal in New York. Cable connections have yet to reach the majority of New York City residents, but Manhattan is fully wired, as are small areas of outer boroughs Brooklyn and Queens. Via public access cable, the ATV Corporation serves a smaller segment of the Chinese population, presenting six hours of Chinese-language programming daily. ATV charges $60 for a one-time 15-second spot; long-term rates are variable and based on a charge per second. This rate varies from $1.65 for a 13-week, once-a-week insert to $1.30 for five spots a week for 26 weeks, or four weekly spots over a year's time.

With so much more time to fill, ATV programming ranges widely. A good deal of it is home produced: "a fast moving mix of late-breaking global news, weather, financial reports, investigative reporting on the local scene, plus a judicious combination of cultural, musical, and dramatic offerings in a magazine format," says ATV's breathless promotion sheet.

Between assigned frequency signals and wired-for-cable delivery, there is the special receiver/ adapter—a receiver attachment that unscrambles encoded broadcast signals. CSTV uses this technology to deliver the widest array of Chinese-language programming in the New York metropolitan area. According to sales rep Yvonne Liu, CSTV is on the air daily with 16 hours of programming, expanding to 24 hours on the weekends. Two hours—one of news, one of talk—are produced locally, while the remainder are imported from Taiwan and Hong Kong. Thirty-second spots begin at $50 for a single run; rates are negotiable for long-term advertisers.

CSTV's drawing power among its 10,000 subscribers was demonstrated on Memorial Day 1987, in a special promotion with the Madison Square Garden Bowling Center. On that traditionally slow day

Asian-Language Media

for indoor recreation, the MSG Center offered premiums to a Chinese-speaking audience targeted through CSTV. The result: more than four thousand enthusiasts came out to participate, startling the Garden and delighting the CSTV sales staff.

Independent in its television operation, CSTV is a local radio affiliate of a nationwide network organized by the Sino Broadcasting Corporation. Headquartered in San Francisco, Sino claims exclusivity as "the only broadcasting company on the U.S. West Coast presenting Chinese-language programs on radio, television, and most recently, publication of our own weekly magazine"—this according to its 1986 rate card.

The claim must be read carefully. Sino is indeed the only broadcaster to offer both radio and television programs in Chinese, but their t.v. cablecasts face competition from four different suppliers—each of whom (to make matters more confusing) leases time on the same broadcast channel, Lincoln Broadcasting Company's Channel 26 in San Francisco. And that broadcast channel is itself delivered to homes by several franchised cable carriers in the Bay Area.

Lincoln's Channel 26 is one of two California stations to mine the second-language market (the other, KSCI, is based in Los Angeles). Its daytime programming is entirely in English and is commercially supported; nights and weekends are devoted to the Asian groups and to a variety of European languages, and extend to Arabic as well. The station came on the air with this programming concept in 1976, and has seen the second-language portion increase over the years. "They're very good customers," according to program director Minda Logan. "They've been with the station quite a while."

"They," insofar as Chinese programs are concerned, are four independent operations: Chinese T.V., Overseas Chinese T.V., International Audio-Visual Communications, and Hua-Sheng Broadcasting Corporation. Each buys time and sells advertising on its own. Lincoln has similar arrangements with Japanese and Filipino suppliers, the latter airing two hour-long programs ("Manila, Manila" and "This Week in Manila") for the past six months. Ms. Logan would like to carry Vietnamese programming, but no group has come forward with an offer. The obvious explanation has to do with program origination. All other language groups can draw on the homeland for original programs or pre-dubbed American shows. The Vietnamese cannot.

Nevertheless, Ms. Logan might well look south to find a nominee. Vietnam Television broadcasts half an hour on Saturday mornings over Channel 04-C in San Diego, a cable outlet, and repeats the offering on Saturday evenings over Los Angeles' broadcast Channel 18, KSCI. News, entertainment, special reports, and editorial opinion are squeezed into the 30 minutes, along with commerical spots from the up-and-coming Vietnamese business community in Southern California.

Against similar fragments in Chinese-language channels, Sinocast Radio and Television, a division of Sino Broadcasting Corporation, offers across-the-board access to the large and economically potent Bay Area Chinese community. According to Sinocast's cable carrier, the Viacom Cablevision Company, 25 percent of its 85,000 cable-wired homes are ethnic Chinese—double the percentage of Chinese in San Francisco's population, and testament to the community's higher earning power and educational levels.

By Sinocast's own count, 40,000 Chinese tune in daily to its radio broadcasts, which began in 1977. The

Sinocast signal goes out by FM subcarrier license; plug-in adapters are rented or bought. Broadcasting is daily, from 9 a.m. to midnight, with the standard mix of music, drama, and news. The vital statistical claim: 70 percent of the audience *never listens to English-language stations*. This creates "a particularly loyal, condensed, and attentive group," Sinocast points out in a neatly packaged media kit, and pledges that "advertising messages broadcast over its channel will undoubtedly register faster and far more effectively."

Sinocasting plans expansion to a nine-city network in the fall of 1987. New York, Los Angeles, San Francisco, Chicago, and Washington will join four Canadian cities in spanning the continent with subcarrier signals, requiring radio adapters.

A DIFFERENT CASE

Chinese and Korean communications groups offer potential advertisers an entry to immigrant populations and a young, native-born generation. Fuji Television takes another tack in promoting its Japanese-language programming. It emphasizes its affluent audience of Japanese businessmen and their families, who are in the States to represent their companies for an average four- to five-year stay.

"Approximately 50 thousand Japanese nationals, making up about 15 thousand families, live in New York," reads the sell letter from Lisa Kyoko Isobe of Fujisankei Communications International (FCI), the Japanese communications giant which also holds Japan's Nippon Broadcasting System. "The income level indicates that they represent a comfortable style of living . . . upon their return to Japan, they are expected to be leaders in their respective fields."

"Most Japanese businessmen are in their late 30s . . . with an average family of four," a viewer profile states. "The average monthly salary ranges around $3,037 before taxes, amounting to $36,450 a year; their living standard is quite high." Indeed, that rate is significantly higher than the impressive median income for Japanese-American households. But Japanese-Americans, so many sources state, are entirely integrated into the American mass market. As a result, Fuji Television and its major competitor, U.S. Nippon Communications, pump the transient population to potential advertisers.

Both enterprises lease time from New York's WNYC, the city-owned public-television station that broadcasts over UHF Channel 31. Fuji supplies two hours of entertainment, news, and cultural fare every weekday morning; U.S. Nippon leases two hours on Sunday evenings and fills it with much the same mix. Both produce local programs to supplement shows purchased from the homeland. Fuji's morning show, "Ohayo, New York," features a "Toyko-New York Hot Line," which connects Fuji's Tokyo news desk with the New York audience. "We consider it a showcase for Fuji t.v.'s best programs," the media kit boasts.

Both enterprises carry ads for Japanese consumer goods. Fuji lists Japan Air Lines, Minolta, Kirin Beer, Maxell Tape, and Toyota as sponsors; U.S. Nippon boasts Nissan, Toyota, Suntori, Sieko, and Toshiba as well as Pan American Airlines and Olympus Airlines. Fuji has different rate structures for its news and entertainment programs, the latter a bit less expensive and available in smaller blocks. A one-time 30-second spot on entertainment programming between 8: 10 a.m. and 9:00 a.m. can be had for $250, and single weekly inserts over a six month period costs $4,680—an average of $180 per showing. News spots, in the previous hour, are sold on a minimum one-month basis. A single showing every weekday—20 spots in a month—costs $4,000, a $200-per-spot average.

Fuji offers production assistance to local advertisers, charging a minimum of $2,000, and also pledges help "if there is any need for a commercial for the New York audience to be produced in Japan." Fuji also gets involved in local promotions, among them a Sumo wrestling tournament and a variety of benefits.

9
Focus on an Asian-Language Agency

GROWTH AND COMPETITION among Asian-language agencies is inevitable, as more corporations seek to take advantage of market dynamics. A third insurance company is currently making plans to gain a foothold; a major food packager is testing the waters with prelimary research; AT&T is actively marketing in Chinese. Soon-to-come developments in cognac marketing call for close attention.

Seminal trends for national campaigns are set in New York, rather than the West Coast. At the moment, the two most prominent agencies serving the market (prominence judged on the basis of national accounts handled) are L3, highlighted in Chapter 6, and Lee and Liu, the focus of this chapter. (In addition, various Chinese-language freelancers are available to serve major uptown agencies.)

In both cases, the material presented is intended to illustrate how such agencies approach the market. No endorsement is intended or implied.

"We wish to teach American companies that it's worth their time and money to advertise to the Asian community," says Raymond Lee, founder and chairman of the New York-based Lee & Liu agency. "They think the Asian market will not prove profitable because it's too small. However, we try to teach them about Asian traditions, Asian buying habits and buying power, the growth of the market, and the profit it can net them."

"The Asian-language market is growing fast," adds partner Joseph Liu. "I see Asian products in competition with American products because Asian producers are willing to spend money to advertise in this market, while the American companies are not. After a while, the Asian-language market will demand only those products that advertise to them."

Asked why Lee & Liu Advertising was created, Liu pointed to the limited amount of quality print advertising in the Asian community. Since he and his partner were trained in advertising, and knew the Asian market (particularly the people and the language), they felt they had the knowledge to bring new products into the community.

"Originally, we just wanted to upgrade the advertising and creativity in the Chinese community, but now, because many American companies are starting to realize the importance of the Asian market, we are expanding our focus. We wish to serve as a bridge, bringing American companies to the Asian community, as well as continuing to help the Asian community upgrade its messages.

"We want to help American companies advertise their products to the Asian community, in both the United States and China, in addition to helping corporations in China sell their products here in the U.S. This help encompasses advertising creative, in addition to package design and promotion activity targeted at either the Asian-American market or the Anglo market, depending on their budget."

Liu notes that Chinese clients have no conception of advertising as Americans know it. Advertising is a small classified ad or a poster, and direct mail is unheard of. "It's not necessary for them to place a full-page ad in the *New York Times*, however," he adds. "Other avenues are available."

When developing a campaign, Lee & Liu seeks to create a company's advertising image through a series of steps. The first step: understand the company and its products. Second, research the Asian community in terms of its acceptance of the product. Third, after the company agrees to go ahead with the project, create an advertising budget. The following illustrates Lee & Liu's cost breakdown for an ad campaign in the Chinese and Korean media:

Newspapers: full-page Chinese newspaper per day - $540
1/2 page Korean newspaper per day - $500

Television: Chinese t.v. commercial per 30-second spot - $300
Korean t.v. commercial per 30-second spot - $350

A print ad production that totals $6,500 includes:
- concept/copywriting
- layout/comps
- Chinese and Korean translation (based on 200 words per ad)
- Chinese and Korean typesetting (based on 200 words per ad)
- mechanicals

A t.v. production of a 30-second spot that totals $20,000 includes:
- concept
- story board
- copy writing
- director
- camera
- actors
- dubbing and technical crew

"When we create a campaign concept, we think bilingual," Lee explains. "How will it sound in both English and Chinese or Korean? Most agencies create a campaign in English first, oftentimes running into problems in the translation stage. Our ads are created using a bilingual mindset, in order to create a bridge between the generations. In many instances, our ads contain copy in both English and Chinese, thereby allowing all generations to view the ad and retain the concept."

Lee & Liu creates both national and local campaigns, with the Asian language market making up 60 percent of their billing, the balance coming from general market ads. In the future, the plan is to concentrate their creative more in Asian-language advertising.

The majority of its work in the Asian-language market thus far has been geared toward the Chinese and Koreans. According to Lee & Liu, the Chinese are more aware of how they appear in ads than the Koreans. They are more concerned that they are perceived as having a professional image.

As yet, they haven't worked with the Japanese, Vietnamese or Filipinos. Their thinking is that most of the Japanese who come to this country are highly educated but travel within the framework of a Japanese company, which functions as an extended family. They tend to remain within the confines of the company and loyal to their homeland, so advertising to them in their native language is not as critical as it is for other Asian groups.

The Filipinos also speak English and assimilate easily into the American culture. An interesting fact about this group is that it carries Hispanic thinking and behavior and can be targeted the same as the Hispanic market. The Vietnamese are the newest group of Asians to migrate to the United States and to Lee & Liu that market, at least right now, is rather small and unassuming.

"In the next two to three years at least, I don't see the Vietnamese market as being very lucrative at all," says Liu. "Their low income status and lack of buying power doesn't appeal to most companies. The Koreans were in the same position when they first came here. Now they are a profitable part of the Asian marketplace."

NEW YORK LIFE INSURANCE COMPANY

Lee & Liu's biggest account to date is New York Life, which has hired the agency to do an entire campaign targeted at the Asian market, primarily the Chinese and Korean communities.

New York Life realized the potential of the Asian market and wanted in. The campaign took seven months to plan and develop, with an annual budget of $300,000, and was designed in three distinct stages. First, a Chinese New Year greeting ad appeared in newspapers this past January, wishing the Chinese and Korean communities a "Happy New Year" and telling them "New York Life is coming to you" in their native languages.

Next came the ads to recruit Chinese and Korean sales representatives. The concept for these ads was direct. According to the partners, they wished to create a simple image that was easy to read and understand. The ad had "New York Life" in bold letters and then listed ten reasons why it pays to join the company. According to Eileen Stroud, senior co-op advertising assistant for New York Life, after these ads first appeared in March 1987, New York Life received approximately 900 responses (700 Chinese and 200 Korean), with more expected.

During the creation of these recruitment ads, Lee & Liu went into the Chinese and Korean communities for feedback on clarity. If the response was negative, the agency went back and changed copy. One problem they encountered was "New York Life" can't be translated into Korean; it doesn't sound right, so it was left in English.

The third and final stage, which debuted at the end of June, featured print ads and t.v. commercials promoting New York Life and its products. Unlike the recruitment ads, the Chinese and Korean concepts were done separately because, in this instance, what appeals to the Chinese people doesn't appeal to the Koreans. "The Chinese and Korean cultures don't mix. The Chinese are more up-scale and sophisticated, and the Koreans are more down to earth and hard working," Lee explained.

The Chinese ad is bilingual so the whole family (older and younger generations) can understand and talk about it. It depicts a lone sailboat drifting in a vast ocean and the caption reads: "If you're searching for financial security, you don't have to sail alone." Here, Lee & Liu wanted to create a sentimental feeling. According to Liu, Asians, especially Chinese, relate to the lone boat because it symbolizes a feeling of being set apart from all others. "The boat says to them, 'You're the immigrant, you're all alone in a strange port, how are you going to plan your future?'"

Because most Koreans are first generation and there is a language barrier, ads targeted to them are in Korean only. The Koreans are more conservative; they love their language and their heritage. "Generally speaking, most Korean parents, especially the mother, don't speak English at all," Liu said. "Most aren't professionally established yet and a lot of them own fish or grocery stores."

This is the image presented in the Korean ads. One portrays a fish-store owner and his family, and another portrays a grocery-store owner and his family. The caption on these ads says: "You're very successful in your business now and you have a family—how are you going to protect them?"

Both the Chinese and Korean ads were slated to run through November 1987, coinciding with 30-second commercial spots on Chinese and Korean t.v. stations. Lee & Liu have engaged 8 Chinese newspapers, 4 Chinese magazines, 11 Korean newspapers, 6 Chinese t.v. stations, and 5 Korean t.v. stations, and estimate an ad will appear in all the media combined on the average of every other day. These stages represent a one year campaign. New York Life's account will help push Lee & Liu's total agency billings to about $750,000 for 1987.

TINNY BEAUTY INC.

Tinny Beauty, Inc., is one of Lee & Liu's bigger clients and one with which they deal directly. Tinny, a Chinese beauty salon chain headquartered in New York, has three branches in Hong Kong, one in China and one in Los Angeles. The company also imports a French skin care product, Reme Laure. Tinny has been in the United States for three years, and Lee & Liu has created a full soup-to-nuts campaign for Tinny for the past two years.

The initial target for Tinny Beauty was the Chinese in America. Full page ads costing $15,000 a month were placed in Chinese newspapers. Magazines and some t.v. and radio stations were also used on a weekly or daily basis. The concept promoted the image of the company and its owner, Lydia Leung, who is a beauty expert. A Korean campaign is currently on the drawing board, according to Tinny's manager, Alex Cheung.

Tinny Beauty also plans on entering the American market sometime this summer. Lee & Liu will handle this campaign as well. The concept here will be to promote Reme Laure, not Tinny Beauty, because Leung feels the Tinny concept wouldn't catch on initially in the American market. If Reme Laure is received well, then perhaps in the future Tinny will promote itself and its owner.

Cheung explained that his company measures the success of the ad campaign by surveying its customers. Coupons on the print ads contain forms asking where a person heard about the company. In this way, Tinny can see which of their advertising methods is most effective.

ADVICE

When placing ads, Lee & Liu advises its clients that print ads are the most effective: about 70 percent more effective. This is because they best transcend the language barrier, and most Asian immigrants read newspapers more than they watch t.v. or listen to radio.

Radio is considered more effective than t.v. because it is available for more hours during the day. Many Chinatown factory workers listen to the radio while they work. Also, most Asian t.v. stations are only carried by cable and not as accessible to the average Asian immigrant.

Companies wishing to target the Asian market should be aware of several major factors. All Asians *do not* understand Chinese. To fully capture the entire Asian market, Lee & Liu advises separate campaigns in the native language of each Asian group being targeted.

An ad portraying the cultural background of the ethnic group being targeted is more appealing, as is one with flashy photographs, catchy headlines, and easy-to-understand copy.

Asian versus American buying habits also have to be considered. Asians are more country loyal than they are brand loyal. Even though they may have been living here for many years, they still feel the United States is not their home. In the same vein, the second generation in the United States is more concerned with its future and that of its children.

"A good example of Asians being country loyal rather than brand loyal would be Campbell's Soup," said Lee. "Campbell's advertises in Hong Kong. The trend over there is to buy Campbell's Soup because it's an American product, and there's a certain degree of pride and status attached to buying foreign products. However, if these same people were to move to the United States, they would no longer use Campbell's Soup, but would use a soup from Hong Kong. Their feeling is it shows loyalty to their homeland."

This raises the question of whether Asian products are a source of competition for American products. Liu feels they definitely are and that some may even beat out American products because the Asians are familiar with them. "If you walk into a Korean food store," he said, "You see shelves of Korean brand products. As long as these products are available, the Asians will buy them. If American companies don't advertise to the Asians in their languages, they definitely lose a piece of the action."

Most of the big-name companies are known to the Asian immigrants prior to their arrival in the United States. Local advertising will reinforce their memory and close the language gap. Asians like to deal

Focus on an Asian-Language Agency

We asked Lee & Liu Advertising Agency what specific types of companies they suggest should advertise to the Asian community. The following represents their list.

Household appliances: because many immigrants leave these items behind when they migrate to the United States.

Banks: especially the smaller savings banks that are located in areas that have a large Asian population.

Financial services, real estate: because of high earning power among the Asians and a strong interest in buying homes or condos.

Insurance: because of the desire to insure their own future and that of their children. In particular, to make sure they have enough money to provide their children with a well-rounded education.

Credit cards: Asians are suspicious of credit cards, since they do not understand the credit system. They are used to paying cash for every transaction.

Cosmetics: because Asian women are conscious of appearance, and for this particular item look for brand names.

Alarm systems: because Asians are very worried about the security of their homes.

Telephone services: to compete with local Chinatown companies.

Soft drinks: to compete with Asian soft-drink companies.

Liquor, beer, cigarettes: to compete with Asian companies.

Food products: to appeal to the second generation who will help the first generation with their shopping. First-generation immigrants are not aware of which products to buy.

Automobile dealerships: because of the high interest among Asians in owning their own cars.

Couriers: to make small Chinatown businesses aware of their services.

Public service announcements: this important information is currently available only for the English- and Spanish-speaking audiences.

with big companies that advertise in their own languages. In this case, familiarity breeds respect.

Both Raymond Lee and Joseph Liu are very optimistic that the Asian market has an extremely bright future. "The education level of the Asians is going up; we're learning more about the American market, and that means we're expecting more," Lee said. "One-third of the Asian population now has a college education, as compared to only 17 percent of the American population."

The message is clear: the Asian market is rapidly growing, and American companies should include it when planning second-language advertising campaigns.

"It's a simple psychology," Liu explained. "More and more immigrants are coming here every year, and most of them have no knowledge of American products. They will choose a product whose advertising they can relate to and understand.

"Once they buy a product and use it, they will continue to use it, and their children and their children's children will use it, and so on. From just one person reading an ad and adopting a product, a company can expect at least four or five others to use it just from that one person. If a company doesn't advertise to the Asians in their language, they stand to lose a large share of the market in the future because the Asian community will learn about its product after they have already chosen and become used to another one.

"My advice to American companies is: There is a definite need to grab the immigrants now because once they're established and have more money, they will buy your product."

And what type of companies in particular should market to the Asians? Liu strongly advises companies that sell financial services and necessary products, such as furniture, appliances, kitchenware, and the like, to advertise to the Asian community, because most immigrants who come here don't bring these things with them from home. Their initial purchases are influenced by what they hear from friends and relatives who have already settled here and by ads they can understand.

An ad in their native language is more appealing to them. It shows a particular company truly values their business and is sensitive to the fact that they have a language problem. It's a nice welcome into a strange country when you see something in your native language.

"It's no longer a question of how many Asians there are living in America, but whether or not American companies wish to compete in the Asian marketplace by marketing directly to the Asians. Even though the market is small, I believe the Asian population will increase 100 percent in the next five to ten years."

This can mean only good things for American companies who wish to reap the benefits of this fruitful marketplace, and for Lee & Liu who plan on expanding their Asian marketing focus.

"Our agency and the Asian market are both growing," Lee said.